Winning Tennis

Books by Scott Perlstein

Winning Tennis
Winning Doubles
Essential Tennis

Winning Tennis

SCOTT PERLSTEIN

The Lyons Press

Photographs by Leslie Katz Josepher
Design by Alessandra Z. Radman, V&M Graphics, Inc.

Printed in the United States of America

10 9 8 7 6 5 4 3 2 1

Library of Congress Cataloging-in-Publication Data

Perlstein, Scott.
    Winning tennis / Scott Perlstein ; edited by Joanne McConnell.
        p.   cm.
    ISBN 1-55821-900-5
        1. Tennis—Psychological aspects.   I. McConnell, Joanne.
    II. Title.
    GV1002.9.P75P47   1999
    796.342′2—dc21   98-48034
                                                                          CIP

Special thanks to Karen Woodell, Chris Pavone, and Joanne McConnell

This book is dedicated
to the memory of my buddy
Tim Gullikson.

Contents

Foreword by Tom Gullikson   ix

Introduction   xl

Chapter 1: The Goals of Practicing   1

Chapter 2: Practice   15

Chapter 3: Shot Mechanics   27

Chapter 4: Game-Plan Strategy   47

Chapter 5: Physical Conditioning   63

Chapter 6: Mental Conditioning—Attitude, State of Mind, Heart, and Fortitude   71

Chapter 7: Match Preparation   83

Chapter 8: At the Match   91

Chapter 9: Key Match Concepts   105

Chapter 10: The Match   119

Chapter 11: Postmatch Analysis   125

Conclusion   133

Acknowledgment   137

Index   139

Foreword

I have always been keenly interested in the mind and its connection to playing competitive tennis at the highest level. As the current United States Davis Cup captain, the highlight of my coaching career was winning the Cup against Russia in the 1995 final. Pete Sampras put on an incredible display of physical and mental toughness in Moscow on red clay, against a very talented Russian team, and had to overcome many hurdles leading us to this historic victory. My twin brother and Pete's friend and coach Tim Gullikson was battling brain cancer. Pete was tired after a long year and he was playing on his worst surface. He won his first match over Andrei Chesnokov 6-4 in the fifth set, collapsing on the clay after hitting a forehand winner on match point with full body cramps. After a full night of therapy and rest I decided to put him in the doubles with Todd Martin, and they beat Kafelnikov-Olhovsky in straight sets to give us a 2-1 lead. On the final day Pete played the best match of his life on red clay, and beat the French Open champion Kafelnikov in straight sets to clinch the victory for the United States. Pete's tremendous effort that cold weekend in the middle of a Russian winter will go down as one of the greatest performances ever in the storied history of the Davis Cup.

I'm the current USA Tennis Director of Coaching for the USTA's restructured Player Development Program, and I'm always searching for ways of communicating the importance of the mind and its vital connection to winning to our coaching staff and our top juniors throughout the country. Teaching our juniors how to compete in an increasingly competitive world game is one of our coaching staff's top priorities. Scott Perlstein's book *Winning Tennis* hits this nail on the head. Many players have lofty goals, but few set out a program to reach their goals. Scott provides you, the competitive player, with a step-by-step program designed to help you maximize your tennis potential. He stresses the importance of a systematic, structured practice plan. He talks about the importance of match preparation and having a good game plan when you walk on the court. He also highlights the importance of being flexible during a match, and having the ability to adjust your game. Finally, he talks about the postmatch program, and how it is important to learn from your wins and losses.

Reading this book will give you a tremendous guideline to follow when developing your own game plan to achieving excellence in our great lifetime sport of tennis. Make a good game plan, enjoy the hard work along the way, and have some fun!

—Tom Gullikson

Introduction

Tom Peters, Robert Covey, and others have written of the mind-set that is necessary to be successful in any endeavor. *Winning Tennis* will show you the mind-set you need to learn to win playing tennis. By closely studying the habits of successful tour pros and teaching instructors, I have come up with the formulas necessary to ensure success on the tennis court. I am going to illustrate the areas you must understand in order to achieve success and what you must think and know. By following the concepts presented, you will be able to successfully handle the psychological and physical pressures that the challenge of competitive tennis presents.

The purpose of this book is to give you a working computer. I will show you how to stay focused on your only goal: developing your tennis mind. George Seifert, the former San Francisco Forty-Niners coach, said that the most important thing he learned from his predecessor, Bill Walsh, was to do nothing that distracts you from your goal of winning. You must learn to eliminate the distractions that can make you mentally unfocused on your goal. In this book, you will learn how to do this.

John Madden, another former football coach, now a commentator, said that you must have a goal. You must know where the finish line is or you will never know when you get there. Our goal is quite simple: learn the structure for success in each step along the tennis process.

Young and even experienced players are often not sure of the full picture of success or the increments to achieve it. To have the success desired you must have no holes in the process that you follow. From shot technique and practice time to the areas in which you must become your opponent's superior to match preparation, equipment, court and conditions of the day, match play, and postmatch analysis, the big picture of structure for success will be presented in easy-to-understand and realistic increments.

CHAPTER 1

The Goals of Practicing

Jimmy Connors, one of the top players ever, explained that tennis is 90 percent mental. In the play *Master Class* by Terrence McNally, the Maria Callas character says, "All nervousness means is a lack of confidence and a lack of preparation." So how do you acquire the confidence? How do you prepare? How do you attain the 90 percent edge?

Your practice sessions enable you to develop the habits that you will need to draw upon to achieve success in a pressure match. Time in and time out, when a professional sports coach is fired, the complaint often raised is that the practice times were not well spent, either overworking or underworking the players, or that practice did not prepare the players for the upcoming battles.

Everything Relates to Every Thing

In 1996, PBS produced a series on learning music, hosted by Wynton Marsalis. One of the shows featured Yo-Yo Ma, the world-renowned cellist, and both musicians explained their goals of practicing. Their final point, which I would like to begin with, is to look for the connection in things. Everything relates to every other thing; the connections necessary to learn music are the same as those to learn tennis. And connections you make in your life, in all areas, heighten your experience and learning process.

I do not limit my growth potential in tennis to what only tennis can teach me. With everything I hear and read in my everyday life, I find a way to relate the new information to what I do and how it could add to my growth in tennis. Furthermore, I am constantly relating things I hear from other coaches in other fields to the tennis that I teach. The key is to have the "computer" in your head switched on at all times. Listen to what others in different fields have learned about how to achieve success. Then figure out how to relate that lesson to your game.

Learn How to Learn

A major part of any practice program is to receive good-quality instruction. In tennis, all the touring pros have a coach. Only a fool thinks he has all the information that he will ever need. And to find a good instructor, you yourself must be ready to learn, and be ready to learn *how* to learn. Learning requires that you picture the end goal and then that you learn how to break down that "march toward the goal line" into small, achievable increments.

In trying to teach new elements of the game to some of the tennis pros on tour, I often notice that these people did not receive enough formal schooling, so they do not know *how* to learn. Whether you're learning math, science, or tennis, there is a step-by-step process required to add knowledge to your brain to improve something that requires constant improvement. Tennis is similar to a business; you must run as fast as you can just to stay even. If you wish to advance, you must run even faster. If you cannot assimilate new information, you will not advance or grow at all.

You must not only want to win, you must also want to learn. Recently, one pro basketball team has been playing below their capabilities because their top three players are not into learning. They view each criticism and suggestion as a personal attack, and resist coaching. They don't understand the difference between their jobs and the coach's job. The players' job is to learn; the coach's job is to teach. If you find your teacher is a poor teacher or is not communicating with you, *on your level,* find a new teacher. Do not assume that learning something new is not for you.

Learn How to Grow

One of the key elements to learning how to grow in tennis is to find a quality coach. How to find the right teacher requires a keen consumer approach by you. You need to find an instructor who thinks tennis is still important, who cares about the game of tennis and his own game enough to have a fire in his belly about the tennis process, someone who is motivated; hopefully, his fire will light yours.

New players come to the game and invent new techniques, and with technological changes in equipment, they also have the ability to change shots. John McEnroe changed serve stances; Andre Agassi is changing the serve-return concept; Pete Sampras changed the serve start position. The new racquets enable the masses to make a shot that only the pros had the skill to hit.

With the ongoing changes in the sport, you need to find a coach who stays current. To stay current, I believe a coach—and you, as a player—should go see the pros in person at tournaments and play competitive tennis. I attend at least one Grand Slam tournament per year, the U.S. Open, and usually I visit the French Open every other year. I also attend one Super Nine, the *Newsweek* Championship, and the two Northern California men's and women's tour events. By seeing the pros in action, I stay on top of the latest trends in the game, and I'm able to relate them to my students. Since I still play competitive tennis, I am always enthusiastic about adding other dimensions to my own game. Thus, I stay current to help both myself and my students. Your instructor should, too.

As a wise consumer, you must figure out how long your coach can help you to grow as a player. Because of their lack of growth, many coaches are able to satisfy only a certain level of player or for a certain period of time. A good teacher is always working on adding new information to his teaching program so he will never run out of things to teach you. Unfortunately, many teachers are not this serious about their tennis or their teaching. My friend Marty Davis, a former ATP tour player, explained why most students jump around from coach to coach: "You stay with the coach until you feel he has given you all the information he has, then you move on." Thus, you must constantly reexamine your coach-student relationship to evaluate the growing process. In all sports, it is common to fire the coach if the team is not progressing satisfactorily. But you must always ask yourself: is it the coach, or is it me? If you feel the coach has more to offer, stay with his program. If you feel you've mastered his program, move on.

One element of good instruction is sharing the same goals and working toward those goals together. You and your instructor should be on the same page of the learning book. You would not hire a tutor who specialized in training students to enter medical school if you wished to attend law school, because the work necessary to pursue each endeavor would be different; you would not be a good student for that tutor, nor would he be the right instructor for you and your goal.

The last element of finding a quality instructor includes finding someone whom you respect. One of the greatest problems in all professional sports today is that the players' earnings far exceed the coaches'. When the coach tells the player something that the player doesn't want to hear or do, the player then insists on a new coach. A friend of mine, David Lee, played basketball in the ABA and was a great free-throw shooter. He has a friend who works in the front office of the Golden State Warriors, the Bay Area's NBA team. When he offered to teach the players how to improve their free throws, which were dismal, he was told that the team would never listen to him, as the players would not view him as a current expert. Although the players could have learned a great deal if they had respected my friend, it was for the best that they did not hire him: since they didn't respect him, they wouldn't have paid attention to his advice. In your own tennis development, there is no point hiring someone you think doesn't know enough, or someone you do not respect.

Set Up a Work Schedule

One of the main goals of this book is to provide you with the structure you need to learn to win. If you are to have any chance at success in any endeavor, you must make time to be successful. I often compare tennis training to studying for an exam in school. I ask my students to tell me about a class in which they are doing well, asking how many hours they spend in class and how many doing homework. Usually they spend at least four times as many hours *preparing for* class as they spend *in* class. No less an effort can be made on the court if you are to succeed. You cannot be inconsistent in the preparation and expect to achieve consistent results.

To set up the proper work schedule, you must first determine your destination goal.

For Juniors:

The first goal is to learn lifetime skills.

The second goal is to achieve a level of success that would allow for the participation on junior high and high school teams.

The third goal is to achieve a state ranking in the juniors age group.

The fourth goal is to train for college tennis.

The fifth goal is to train for the pro circuit.

For Adult Players:

The first goal is to learn lifetime skills and add a social aspect that tennis interaction allows.

The second goal is to play on a club team and in leagues.

The third goal is to reach a high USTA rating.

The fourth goal is to play in state ranked tournaments.

The fifth goal is to play in national and international tournaments.

To achieve these goals, both juniors and adults must add conditioning time and a visual learning period to their preparation routine.

Conditioning Time

The player needs to increase her conditioning as her work schedule increases. As she plays more matches with greater frequency, she must be in shape to withstand playing long matches, sometimes two in one day, for a couple of days in a row.

After Pete Sampras lost in the first round 1996 U.S. Open, with his lack of fitness being the primary cause, he hired a fitness guru to work him into better shape. The guru felt Sampras rated only a four on the conditioning scale of ten. Together, they embarked on a twice-daily ninety-minute nonstop workout, including sprints on the track, sprints on the court, stationary bike work, stomach crunches, and medicine-ball work. All serious players must include running, stretching, weights, and strengthening work in their regimen.

The more serious you are about increasing your level of play, the more serious you must be about training. You can make up your own training regimen or hire a personal trainer to design a program for you to follow. Either way, the program needs to be upgraded on a regular basis, at least every six months, to increase your conditioning and strength.

Visual Learning

Some people learn better verbally, others sensually; still others learn better visually. Regardless of which is best for you, watching pro tennis on television and in person is critical to your growth and development in tennis. Observe the mechanics of the pros and follow their court strategies. The fact that you don't have the arm talent of the pros doesn't make their matches less relevant to your growth. Understand how the pro game relates to your game. Break down the pieces of the shots so you can learn how those pieces are applied by the pros.

One of my newer adult students told me he had never watched pro tennis until he started taking lessons from me. He didn't understand how the pro game was relevant to his. Now that he's trying to copy the pro game, he watches at every opportunity because he knows what to look for. The television commentators sometimes don't understand this concept. During the finals of the 1997 Grand Slam Cup, one of the commentators claimed that the average player cannot relate to how Sampras was playing. I disagree. All serious players can easily relate to how Sampras was playing. It was clear what his serve motion was, what his stroke-and-volley methods were, and how he had improved his serve-return technique. The fact that the average player cannot *duplicate* those skills should in no way discourage the player from trying to emulate the method.

Matches are shown on television all the time. If you are fortunate enough to live in an area where the pro tour plays, make it a point to attend the matches. In person, it is even easier to see the shot technique that you are trying to copy. My form is very sound, but I never think of my shots as my own because I am copying Edberg's backhand, Sampras's forehand and serve, and Rafter's volley. When I miss a shot, I close my eyes and run the video of the shot I am trying to copy. I attend many tour events to refresh my videos of the pros and to make sure there isn't a more current or better video to copy.

Your Own Video

You should be making and studying videos of your match play. At the 1997 U.S. Open, I spoke with Jim

Loehr, the noted sports psychologist, as we watched a match together. I asked him why videos weren't used as much in tennis as they were in so many other sports. He explained that studies have shown that in golf and tennis, too much video self-analysis makes the player overthink, which causes them to lose some of the spontaneity that makes them great performers. But he does recommend videotaping some matches and, most important, making a compilation video of your greatest hits, which you should study all the time.

Because it is often difficult for a player to remember the specific points of a match, a video replay can provide important information. Videos can facilitate discussion and observation of how the shots and strategies worked or failed. Since many of my students can't pay me to watch them play, they will have a friend or relative videotape their matches; I can view the tapes later, and then discuss them during the lessons. The videos help me see how the student performs under stress. As a coach, I find the use of videos under these circumstances very helpful.

The Work Schedule for Juniors

To achieve the first goal, learning lifetime skills, a junior needs to devote a seasonal three months to tennis instruction and playing with friends or family. Ideally, he'll schedule a one-hour tennis lesson once per week, combined with two or three one-hour hitting sessions per week. This seasonal dabbling over a period of years will pique the interest of the child to advance on the learning goal ladder.

To achieve the second goal, making a school team, a junior needs to be involved in a year-round lesson program. For at least six months, the serious tennis student should be playing and practicing at least three times per week. At this level, conditioning programs must be introduced, which can include other sports, especially soccer, basketball, track, and cross-country running. All of these activities should include stretching and strength workouts. At least once a month, the junior should be watching a pro match on television to help him with the visual learning.

To achieve the third level, a state ranking for tournament play, a junior needs to be involved in a year-round lesson program. For at least eight months, the student should be taking lessons, practicing, and playing at least three times per week; during the tournament season, playing and practicing is a five-day-per-week commitment. The junior needs to participate in a major tennis camp for at least one week per year. He needs to ascertain the minimum number of tournaments played that's needed to achieve a state ranking, normally five to seven, and should play at least three more than the minimum. Four days per week must include at least a half hour of conditioning work. And at least three times per month, the junior should be watching a pro match on television or in person.

To achieve the fourth level, playing college tennis, the junior should still be enrolled in a year-round lesson program. The junior must achieve a state ranking. During the tennis season, he should be playing and practicing four days per week; during the tournament season, he should be playing and practicing six days per week. The junior needs to participate in a major tennis camp for at least two weeks. If the goal is a major Division I, top-twenty ranked school, the junior should start playing some regional and national tournaments, whose eligibility requires a high state ranking. Four days per week must include at least one hour of conditioning. And at least four times per month, the junior should be watching a pro match on television. This player should also be studying videos of his matches at least once per week and should also have a video of his greatest hits for regular review.

To achieve the last level, becoming a touring tennis pro, there are two avenues to pursue: high-level college tennis as a stepping stone to a pro career, or a full-time tennis camp. Some juniors go to school for a short period, then turn pro, as did John McEnroe. Such a player may win the NCAA championship and feel there is nothing left to be achieved at the college level, so he may opt for professional tennis. Others stay in school to earn a degree before turning pro. Richey Reneberg graduated from Southern Methodist University and became the number one player in the world in doubles. MaliVai Washington graduated from the University of Michigan and became a top ten player in singles.

If the student chooses to enroll in a full-time tennis camp, there are four or five camps in this country that specialize in producing pros, including two owned by the International Management Group. In Germany, Boris Becker owns a camp. In these situations, the work schedule is set for you; then it is up to you to expand upon the workload.

The Work Schedule for Adults

To achieve the first goal, learning lifetime skills, the adult needs to devote a three-month season to learning the sport. The adult should take one lesson per week, and hit with friends at least twice per week. Hopefully, like the junior player, after enough dabbling the tennis bug will kick in, creating a desire to attain higher goals.

To achieve the second level, playing on club teams and with friends, the adult needs to devote a six-month season to playing tennis. During this season, one lesson per week is needed, and hitting with friends should occur at least twice per week. As matches are being played, a year-round conditioning program must be started, with a minimum of at least three times per week devoted to twenty-minute workouts. This adult should start to watch at least one pro match per month and should have a video of her shots to examine.

To achieve the third level, climbing the USTA number ladder, tennis must become a year-round sport. The USTA has devised a numeral rating system, 1 through 7, to help standardize a player's tier: 1 is a beginner and 7 is a touring professional; league levels start at 2.0 and go to 5.5. This adult needs to take lessons once per week and play in quality games at least three times per week, pushing the development of skills. The player needs to be involved in a year-round conditioning program consisting of a workout at least three days per week, a half hour minimum. This adult should be watching at least three pro matches per month and studying videos of her game at least once per month. The player must also be regularly reviewing her greatest-shots video.

To achieve the fourth level, playing state tournaments, tennis must be a year-round sport. This player needs to be involved in a lesson program once per week or, if skill level is beyond the local tennis instruction available, studying the pros all the time. This adult must play at least three times per week in high-quality games and be involved in conditioning work six days per week. Also, the player should be watching pro matches as often as possible. This adult should make and study a video of her game once a month and frequently study a compilation tape of her greatest hits.

To achieve the fifth level, playing national and international tournaments, tennis is a year-round sport. The workout program is the same as the local tournament player. The only difference is that the quality of practice opponents must be substantially higher to help prepare this player for the level at which he will compete.

Realistic Goal Levels

It's important that the junior enthusiast have realistic goal levels. Very few juniors have college and pro potential, but for those who do, I stress that they should go for it and not waste the talent that so few have. Realistically, it would be cruel to tell a player who has no chance of achieving that upper level of tennis that he should put the work in to try to get there. However, that junior may achieve a high enough level of proficiency to make the junior-high or high-school team, which, for that player, will be a huge accomplishment.

Adults also must be realistic about the ladder they want to climb. Even starting later in life, one can climb high. What is important, though, is not to skip a level of growth. A 3.0 player over the years may become a national player, but must go through nine more steps and years of play to reach that level. A few years ago, *Sports Illustrated* ran an article about a forty-five-year-old man who decided to take up tennis and become an ATP pro in a few years. He quit his job and was devoting himself full-time to his pursuit. This was a ridiculous endeavor, because even ATP pros are not able to compete at that level once they reach thirty-five. Thus, someone who never reached that level and is ten years older has no chance of ever reaching that goal.

Periodization

It is important to vary more intense periods of training with some downtime, a schedule called periodization. As you prepare for a bigger event or match, you train harder. It is healthy, both mentally and physically, to enjoy some time off to prevent staleness and overtraining. The key to remember during your downtime is to not let so much time go by that you lose your conditioning and some of your tennis skills. When you return after time off you need to create a "spring-training" mentality. Tennis is a live-pitching sport; there is no substitute for the live hitting. Thus, even if you maintained your conditioning, it will take a while before your rhythm kicks in and you properly time your hit. If you understand this, you will be much happier, mentally, when you return.

One of the first pros that Tim Gullikson coached used to return from a short break and be distressed during his first two days back because he felt unpolished and had zero tolerance for less than great practices. If he had returned with a spring-training attitude, he would not have reacted so severely to his temporarily lesser performance.

Tracking Your Development

You should have growth goals and a time frame for those goals. I will set goals for my students for periods of four to six months, at the end of which the goal must be mastered to a point of total confidence. With the mastery will come an increased success rate in playing. It is often difficult for a player to realize and remember where they came from. In my program, I am dealing with many students who compete against one another, and thus they have difficulty measuring their gains since everyone is working on the same thing and improving; they do not see any comparative growth. I tell them to play someone they have not seen in six months, especially someone who they thought was much better. Invariably, they come back and say, "Wow, I didn't realize how far I've come!"

Tennis growth occurs in spurts. First, you master a new element in your game; then there is a stabilization period of the mastery; and finally, your computer brain is ready for more information and growth.

CHAPTER 2

Practice

Concentrate During Practice

You must put all of yourself into practice. This is where you set the tone for your play style. If you don't put forth a concentrated effort here, it is extremely difficult to turn it on for a match. When Magic Johnson coached the Los Angeles Lakers for a short period, he found the lack of practice effort most disturbing. He tried to convey to his young players that when he was part of world-champion teams, they used to practice hard, which carried over to hard play in the games. His players responded by saying it was the nineties, don't worry: although we don't want to practice hard, it's all right because we'll play sound and hard during the game. It turns out that the team could not play sound and hard during the game.

Learning and mastering your shots and play strategies takes time, and it's quite unlikely that the advanced skills necessary to perform can be turned on like a water faucet. Practice sessions in which you are just marking time are useless. Unless you are going to practice with passion and purpose, you are better off not practicing.

The key to concentrating during practice is to practice with a goal; random hitting is not helpful. Many of the high schools in my area have supervisory coaches for the tennis team—the coach is there to merely supervise the kids, not to help them with their tennis. Often, the young players get *worse* during the tennis season instead of better. The reason is simple: practice time is a waste where bad habits of focus and technique are practiced. These carry over to their match play. There are times when you are better off going to the movies than practicing.

It is not the number of minutes spent on the court that is important; it is the purposefulness of those minutes. Pete Sampras said that he and Tim Gullikson used to work a shorter practice time to maximize his participation, and then go play golf. Spending twice the time practicing but only being there mentally for part of it makes for wasted time. Practice is where you "set the table" for your match play: you must learn to stay focused for a long period of time; you must learn to play with a high degree of seriousness. Practice is the place to form these habits.

Every practice should focus on specific growth elements. If you want to improve your backhand, then more hitting drills and serve returns to the backhand would be the order of the day. Keep the practice moving and stimulating by mixing up what you do. Don't wait until you're bored before you move on to the next task.

Understand the purpose of your practice sessions. Work on your shots, strategies, and conditioning because you see it as a part of the march toward success. With a purpose and goal in mind, you will put more into the practice. One of the pros I worked with commented during the practice, "These are great drills;

what do they have to do with playing?" Because this player could not see the needed connection, he was less than enthusiastic about the practice. You must see and understand the connection between the drills and your goal or you will fall into the same trap.

Relax During the Learning Process

Practice slowly, and take your time learning. Learning is achieved through a building-block process, layer upon layer, and there are many layers needed to build a solid foundation. New students often want to jump to step twenty in the process, but it would never stick because they are missing steps nine through nineteen.

Without a strong base upon which to build, you are building a house of cards that will surely tumble down at the first sign of stress. Even at the pro level, you will occasionally see a player break down mechanically. One wonders how this could happen at such a high level. It happens for the same reason it does at a lower level: the pro doesn't have a step-by-step solid foundation of the shot.

Except in a few forums, you are not allowed to be coached on the court. So it is important that you develop the skills to become your own coach. One of my favorite lines is "The form does not fail you; you fail the form." If you miss a shot, you must run the video of the correct shot that is in your head. If you didn't take time to fully master the shot, you will not be able to re-create the vision.

Practice the Harder Elements Longer

Whether you are a 3.0 player or a touring pro, you must believe that you have a degree of mastery of your shots and play strategies. A few years ago at the French Open, one of the players screamed in game three, "There goes my backhand. It's been bad for two weeks, and it's still bad." This player was cooked from that moment on, and got killed in the match. If you are above the 3.0 level and have holes or weaknesses in your game, your opponent will easily figure them out, and unmercifully attack them. Given the weaknesses, you walk on the court afraid, knowing you are unprepared for the battle.

Practice time is when you develop your confidence in your skills. If one skill is escaping mastery, you must practice that more. None of the major skills in tennis is tougher to learn than the others. However, everyone hits ten forehands for every five backhands and every one serve. If you don't take extra practice time to make up this difference, you wind up with a forehand twice as good as your backhand and ten times better than your serve. You can't leave any skills behind. In a recent interview, Sampras said he hits forty extra serves per day at the end of practice. If you hit forty extra serves, five days per week, that's two hundred extra serves per week. Two hundred extra anything per week will greatly facilitate your skill improvement.

Develop a trust in the knowledge level of the skill during practice. Dodging the shot because you don't like to work on it is not going to help you master it. When a shot is tough to master, the difficulty can lead to frustration. Remember to take your time in trying to master the difficult elements, and don't get too impatient with yourself over the seeming lack of progress. Practice time is meant to be the time you work on both strengths and weaknesses.

Charles Hoveler, one of the top senior players in the world, has said it is important that you practice the tough shots because they may come up in a match, and you'll need to make all of them, from backhand overheads and half volleys to dig-out shots off your shoes and many more. You must have practiced your response to difficult incoming shots in order to make them in match play.

I often compare match play to taking an exam. It always amazed me to hear a fellow student say that he hoped the professor did not test on a specific area because he did not study for it. Of course the area was going to be tested; it was part of the program. Walk into every match expecting to be tested on everything.

Expression and Attitude

Always play with a maximum of expression, and always have the proper attitude. This means you must generate the energy, focus, and desire required to play your best in a match. These skills cannot be viewed as water-faucet skills, turned on and off at a moment's notice. In practice, you learn to be successful in the match. If your practice is sloppy and effortless, you will play the same way. At the 1997 *Newsweek* ATP tournament, Richey Reneberg told me that one day he was practicing with a higher-ranked player. He thought it would be a great workout. Instead, he had to keep asking the other fellow if he was all right, if he wanted to stop, because the fellow was just walking through the workout. Obviously, he was not in the mood to practice. Thus, Richey's practice was wasted.

When you are working out with someone and want that person to hit with you again, you are obligated to put forth the necessary effort. It is rare that I encounter someone in a lesson who does not put forth the concentration and effort level I require, since he is paying for the lesson. However, on occasion a person comes in without focus or effort, so I quickly establish the required work ethic. If someone is not up to task, I tell him that I am not his teacher.

Forgive Yourself

Don't be too hard on yourself, and try to learn from your mistakes. In every tournament, everyone loses except one player. Even the top players do not win every match. Thus, one must learn how to turn losing into a positive experience.

A friend once told me that he found tennis extremely frustrating. When he played baseball, he could be perfect. He would catch the six balls that came his way in the game. Often, he would go four-for-four at bat; thus, he never failed. This is one of the superiorities of tennis. In his sport of baseball, he was presented with only ten opportunities to participate. In tennis, you may have ten opportunities to participate during just one point. With so many chances for participation comes an inevitable increase in failure.

Make Missing a Positive Experience

One of the major purposes of practice is to expand your game, to work on new shots and fill the holes in your game. If you have no patience for the learning process, you will drive yourself crazy. During lessons I tell my students that I would rather see them miss the right shot than make the wrong one. You can only learn and improve what you practice. If you are missing, but trying to learn the right technique or placement, you must allow time for growth. Be patient and tolerant. Try to understand why and how you are missing. For example, in trying to hit the underspin drive shot, let's say you floated the shot out. What caused this? You dropped the racquet head on the hit. To make this a positive experience, you would acknowledge the following:

Great for me: I recognized it was the right time to
hit the shot.

Great for me: I aimed the shot correctly.

Minor problem: my execution was off a little bit.
This is not a big problem: I am aware of what
has to be done, and next time I will execute the
mechanics better.

Make Losing a Positive Experience

First of all, you should not be concerned with winning or
losing when you are working on new elements to your
game. Sampras has said that when he is adding something new to his game, he will keep working on that
element in practice even if he is losing or it is not working. For example, he has been working on the second-
service-return chip shot, in the style of Stefan Edberg,
who chipped so well. In his practice sets, Sampras keeps
repeating this tactic, even though it may not be working well, because he knows that the only way to master
a skill is to practice it. Practice your shots under stress-
ful conditions, so that you will become confident
enough to integrate the skill into your game, even
under greater stress.

View your practice sets as an opportunity to push
your limits as much as possible. Do not be concerned
with winning or losing. If your practice sets are tough,
the tournament match may well seem like a vacation.
This is how I practice. My two regular game opponents
are great players. Both Mark Jee, who played for the
Naval Academy, and Dave Luther, who played for James
Madison, are tough as nails. Both fight for every ball on
every point. If I do not put forth maximum effort, I get
run over. Although I try to win every time, I don't care if
I lose. I am trying my hardest, and I know that by play-

ing these two gentlemen, I'm twice as tough as I ever was. In tournaments, I'm relieved to play lesser players. When I meet the top players in my senior division, they only match the toughness that I am used to seeing.

Play the Same and Develop the Proper Attitude

In practice, you set the tone for how you play. Use your practice time wisely to expand your game. However, everything you do should be practiced using your game-face mentality.

Be optimistic and don't complain.

Attitude is important for your success, and you must employ an "I can" attitude. In practice, you are often trying to add to your game, filling some holes. At times, this may be difficult; it is easy to become pessimistic and whine about how tough practice is. But you must believe you are an achiever and will master what you are working on. The skills required to become an upper-level player are difficult to master. Show patience and a positive attitude and give yourself time to grow into what it is you are trying to become—a better player.

Believe You Are a Winner

You must learn to believe you belong on the court with your opponent and deserve to win. In playing tier tennis, you must believe you have a chance to win the match—your practice work has prepared you for the match.

Your winning attitude starts in practice. You must see yourself in a positive light; you are good, and your work will make you successful. If you do not have a long history of winning, it is important that you earn some wins in your practice matches, because winning and losing are contagious. In a close match the player with a better winning history will usually prevail.

Respect Your Opponents

You must believe that your opponent is a deserving adversary and capable of beating you. Boris Becker lost in the first round of the 1997 Australian Open, even though he was the defending champion. You must assume that if the opponent is playing this tournament, he is able to beat you. Do not underestimate any opponent; bring your best game to the court every time.

This attitude also starts in practice: if you've asked someone to practice with you, apply the same work ethic you employ in your regular practice sessions. Focus, even if you think the practice partner is not as good as you; there is always something you can work on.

Work Ethic

Practice is serious business, so do not goof around. Practice with a purpose. One of the pros I worked with had to end practice very early one day because he tried to hit a shot between his legs. He missed the shot and hit his ankle with his racquet, and he limped off the court. To sport a working attitude in match play, it is critical that you practice with the proper attitude.

Learn to Think

Learn to focus and play at the level you have achieved. In all sports, one often hears the phrase "Get your head into the game." When you play, you must constantly draw upon your knowledge and experience base. Act and react using every bit of knowledge you have attained. The more you improve, the more critical it will be for you to draw upon your knowledge when facing a skillful opponent. The better your opponent, the less margin for error.

Review Your Game Plan

Before you play, you must establish your mental game. During play, your computer must be switched on. Observe what is and is not working, then make the necessary adjustments. Analyze the play, and do more of what works. Figure out which of your opponent's weapons is hurting you, and try to shut it down.

I once heard a football coach remark that although he saw something happening, he did not make the adjustment required during the game. Although the observation itself has some merit, it also must be acted upon to influence the results. Just as the coach needed to alter his plan when he initially recognized the problem, you must figure out the adjustments required during the contest and have the confidence and courage to institute them. Learn to think for yourself; train yourself to quickly process information on the court.

Deliver Your Talent

Part of learning to think requires forcing yourself to focus on delivering your capabilities to their highest level. Even for the pros, their most frustrating element is their failure to play at the level they've learned. In most cases, no one is playing poorly on purpose. However, you must reach the point where anything less than an 85 percent performance level is not acceptable. You must develop a strong work ethic in order to deliver what you know.

What puts any player at the top of his tier is the day-in, day-out consistency of producing at his knowledge level from start to finish. If you are making a three-hour business presentation and waste the first twenty minutes fumbling around, trying to get organized, before you finally begin, you will not be effective, and your audience will be dissatisfied and inattentive. If at the two-hour mark you suddenly start talking about things unrelated to your base presentation and waste another thirty minutes before righting the ship and finishing strong with a solid conclusion to your topic, you would probably be fired. Although the above little parable is exaggerated, something similar often happens in tennis, a coming and going of talent. Your job in practice and in matches is to bring along your best for as long as is required.

In order to learn to win, your goal must be to become superior to your opponent in seven areas: shot mechanics, game-plan strategy, conditioning, state of mind, attitude, heart, and fortitude. It is not enough to be strong in only a few of these areas; you must be equal to or better than your opponent in all seven.

CHAPTER
3

Shot Mechanics

At a recent U.S. Open, my friend Dave Luther, while watching a top player with a unique style of hit, said, "It shows that it doesn't matter what style you use, as long as you do it all the time and have mastered it." If you watch pros play, you will notice a difference in technique, up to a point, and although there is no such thing as a right or wrong style, there are six issues you must resolve regarding mechanics: grip, start technique, hit point, rhythm, finish technique, and balance.

Grip

There is much range in the grips used. If there were proof positive that only one grip would work, all players would certainly use that grip. So make yourself comfortable. Know where your grip is and be able to correctly change it from shot to shot. But if your shot is inconsistent, change your basic grip position. When you feel your shots are too weak you may also change from one-handed to two-handed shots, or vice versa. Some players find that to get extra power and increase the ability to absorb powerful shots from the opponent, they need to use two hands. Monica Seles, one of the top women players ever, uses two hands on both forehand and backhand. Pete Sampras as a youth changed from a two-handed backhand to a one-handed backhand, reasoning that because he wanted to be a one-handed volleyer, he would have more consistency on the backhand side using one hand all the time.

Hand Position

Forehand: Stefan Edberg used a continental grip, which is formed by holding your hand in the center of the racquet, on his forehand. Alberto Berasategui uses a western grip, which is formed by rotating the racquet to the forehand side to a point that the hand is almost on the bottom of the racquet. Those two extremes encompass the wide range on the forehand. I do not recommend either of the extremes, but prefer to see most players use a semi-western grip, which is formed by splitting the traditional eastern—formed by shaking hands with the racquet—and the western. The more to the western side your grip is, the easier it is to hit topspin. The more to the continental side, the easier to hit underspin.

 Backhand: Again the range is from the continental to the extreme western. And again the western grip is formed by rotating the hand to the bottom of the racquet on the backhand side. I suggest the student use an eastern grip, which is a slight rotation from the continental grip toward the backhand side, or a semi-western, which rotates ever so slightly more to facilitate hitting both topspin and underspin with the same grip.

Serve: Almost all big-time players hold at least a continental grip, if not a full eastern backhand grip. Holding your grip more to the backhand side greatly facilitates the ability to snap your wrist, which generates more racquet-head speed on the hit.

Volley: Most big-time players hold one grip, the continental grip.

Start Technique

Forehand: All the top players have switched to the double turn of rotating both the racquet and the combination of hip and shoulder. This is achieved by keeping the hand and racquet together on the turn of the shoulders. For a right-hander, if you pull your right elbow back, this is achieved instantly. From this spot, there is a variation on the back swing. Some pros bring the racquet up, some bring it down.

Forehand double turn, key elements: elbow is pulled back, both hands are still on the racquet, racquet is in the preparation set, and hips and shoulders are turned for instant preparation.

*One-handed back-
hand double turn,
key elements: elbow
is pulled back, both
hands are still on the
racquet, racquet is in
the preparation set,
and hips and shoul-
ders are turned for
instant preparation.*

*Two-handed back-
hand double turn,
key elements: rac-
quet, hips, and
shoulders are in
the preparation set.*

Backhand: The preparation used is the same early shoulder and hip turn as the forehand. If as a right-hander you pull your left elbow back, this is achieved instantly. One-handed backhanders have two choices: loop out of the start or "kick the racquet head" tight to the body. The "kick the head" style is the one used most by the pros. The two-handers are dropping the racquet down or kicking the racquet up like the one-handers.

Volleys: The key is the breakout angle of the racquet head. All the top players keep that start spot in front of the body, so the racquet head is still visible on the start, with the racquet head above the wrist.

Forehand volley breakout, key elements: racquet is in front of the hitter in the hitter's sight line, the racquet head is slightly above the wrist at a 90-degree angle.

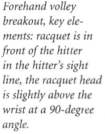

Backhand volley breakout, key elements: racquet is in front of the hitter in the hitter's sight line, the racquet head is slightly above the wrist at a 90-degree angle.

Overhead key elements: hitter has pulled elbow back across shoulder, which forces a turn to the side, knees are bent, eyes up to the ball.

Overheads: Spin out and pull back with the foot on your hitting side, as if you were a quarterback dropping back for a pass, keeping your neck up, which forces your head up even more. The additional key is to hit the bottom of the ball.

Hit Point

The contact point for a controlled hit must be struck out in front of the body. To impart topspin, the racquet must contact the ball low to high, with the face of the racquet as squared up as possible. For underspin, the racquet contacts the ball high to low, with a minor lead of the bottom edge.

Rhythm

When Jim Courier was number one a few years back, he said he hit the ball at 85 percent power. Tiger Woods, the pro golf sensation, says he hits at only 80 percent. If you consider the speed that both of these players generate, you are apt to think that they are kidding, but they are not. There is no question that you must upgrade your hitting rhythm to at least 80 percent and shoot for up to 90 percent. One of the reasons Courier's ranking has slipped is that many players now generate his amount of power or more; they are used to absorbing his shots. Plus, tennis is a first-strike game: if you first strike your opponent hard enough, you will force him into a defensive mode, which makes it tougher for him to strike back at you. When Ivan Lendl was retiring, the same applied to his game. He had gone from being the hardest hitter to just one of the boys. On the women's side of pro tennis the same is true: there used to be only a few hard hitters; now there are fifty.

Finish Technique

On the forehand side, the key concept centers on racquet-head speed. You must accelerate through the hit, either going over your shoulder or up on the same side of your body. Sampras is the current role model, having the best forehand in tennis.

On the backhand side, for two-handers the same two concepts apply, hand and racquet-head speed. Andre Agassi accelerates the racquet so that it goes over his opposite shoulder; the other choice is the quick yank up on the same side. Most of the one-handers still use a power drive through finish, with the racquet accelerating through but going out toward the opponent's side.

Forehand over-the-shoulder finish, key elements: shoulder is to the chin, elbow is inclined higher, racquet goes over the shoulder, showing the opponent the bottom label of the racquet.

Forehand yank-up finish, key elements: high incline of the racquet finish on the same side of the body as the hit.

Backhand over-the-shoulder finish with two hands, key elements: left shoulder to the chin, both elbows up, the left elbow higher than the left shoulder, racquet over the shoulder showing the opponent the bottom label of the racquet.

One-handed backhand topspin finish, key elements: long up-and-out drive finish with the hitting arm inclined so the shoulder is to chin level; the elbow, hand, and racquet head all are inclined up.

Balance

If you can stop before you hit the ball, it will be easier to maintain a balanced body on the hit. The pros, these days, are running through, jumping, and spinning around on some shots. These are advanced maneuvers, but they are still in balance because they keep their head still and their shoulders are on a straight line, aligned with their hips.

Once you're comfortable with the preceding mechanics, address the following run-through-the-ball concepts:

Forehand: When the ball lands extremely wide, it is very tough to pull the hitting arm across the shoulder on the full run. Thus, the hit requires a yank-up technique that loops the topspin. Your follow-through goes out, then up on the same side of your body. When you catch your racquet, you form a triangle. If you can stop, great; if not, just run through the shot. If the ball gets slightly behind you when on the run, the hit then requires a tomahawk slice that pulls the ball back into the court.

Tomahawk slice, key elements: high to low hit, with a drive up-and-out finish.

Backhand: Same concept on the extreme wide ball—the hit is a bigger yank, increasing the low to high hit on the ball to achieve a looped topspin effect. Stopping is not relevant. If the ball gets slightly past you, reach back and wrist the shot back, slicing the shot.

Short Shot: On the extremely short run shot, forehand or backhand, pull the elbow on the hit side back and run with your toes forward, right through the shot, following through with either the topspin or slice shot.

The two key growth concepts on these shots is to forget turning and stopping. By placing your elbow back you will get enough racquet preparation. Make sure on the extreme run that you are hitting with purpose. Don't run just to chase the ball, as this leads to quitting the shot or overrunning the ball.

Run-through short forehand, key elements: same double turn as the basic forehand, toes stay forward and keep on moving.

Run-through short backhand, key elements: same double turn as the basic backhand, toes stay forward, and keep on moving.

This run-through concept also applies to volleys:

Forehand Volley: When the ball floats as you are coming to the net, instead of waiting for the ball to come to you after you have split stepped, attack the volley with a bursting forward run through the shot. Keep your volley form, with no back swing, but move those toes forward.

Backhand Volley: Same exact concept as the forehand volley: burst through the float volley.

Run-through forehand volley, key elements: same start, with the breakout in front of the hitter, toes forward. It is even more critical to keep the racquet in front. If you add more body power and more swing, the shot will go out by twenty feet.

The Serve

This is so important that it has its own section. For over four years I have been encouraging my students to switch to the Sampras service motion. On the pro level more players each year have gone to this style.

Start

The key change of the Sampras service motion occurs at the start. Instead of starting with the weight on the front foot and timing a rocking motion from front foot to back foot to front foot, Sampras eliminated one step. He starts with his weight on his back foot, lifting the front toe off the ground. To achieve power, it is critical that you get your weight onto your back foot, which enables you to push forward on the hit. Sampras correctly intuited that since he had to transfer weight to his back foot anyway, he should simply start there, and cut out the rocking back step. Thus, there is one less part of the serve to execute incorrectly. So park your weight on your back foot to give yourself great balance, then lean into the hit.

Hands

Sampras begins with his hands and racquet together, at about eye level. When he starts his motion, both arms drop down, separating around thigh level. By starting with the racquet up, Sampras lets the racquet drop down by itself, instead of trying to figure out the racquet speed or arm lightness.

Body

After he bounces the ball one time, Sampras stops and holds his "catching the ball" posture, which means his shoulders are over his toes.

Sampras serve start, key elements: front foot up, all weight on the back foot, hands together, waist slightly folded.

The Tossing Arm Motion

This applies to all serving techniques:

1. Same down spot every time.
2. Same up-release point every time.
3. Same rhythm of arm swing.
4. Release ball out through the "top door" of the hand. Sampras says to put the thumb inside your hand. I also recommend that you point all your fingers up to the sky, as if they were being pulled out of your hand. If you stretch your fingers up or squeeze your thumb inside your hand, your wrist won't flip your toss all over the place.
5. Hold the tossing arm up for at least one count, ideally two.
6. Softly collapse the tossing arm across your body.

If you watch the pros, you'll notice that they all maintain a toss-release rhythm and place their tossing hand in a "toss cup" every single time.

I have added two more key points for toss control. First, add a gentle pressure to your fingertips while holding the ball before you start the tossing motion. Maintain this pressure on the ball, then open your hand at the peak of your reach, just enough to let the ball escape skyward. This technique ensures that your tossing hand is positioned perfectly every time.

The second point is to maintain a constant speed of the tossing arm's lift. When the toss is off, it is usually caused by the jarring of the arm as it rises. If you maintain a constant lift speed, this problem is defeated. This correction has been very helpful to many of my students.

Toss, key elements: tossing arm fully extended, fingers to the sky.

Tossing arm finish, key elements: tossing arm softly collapses onto the hitter's body, producing a hugging effect.

Weight Transfer

You must toss the ball while your weight is forward in your stance. With your weight on the back foot in the Sampras start, simply lean into the toss.

Alignment of the Toss Arm

From the folded waist position, begin the service motion by lifting your tossing arm so that the wrist, elbow, shoulder, and hip are all aligned. This alignment ensures that the ball is placed perfectly every time, assuming the weight transfer and swing of the arm are done properly. Stop thinking about delivering the toss. Simply fold your waist and align.

Speed of the Toss Arm

On a scale of ten, with one being no speed and ten the maximum, the arm separation speed should be no more than three. As the ball is released, you want to reach a fast hit speed, a minimum of eight and up to ten. Remember that to achieve more power on the serve, you must accelerate into the hit.

Sampras Bonuses

Shoulders and Hip Rotation: As Sampras leans forward, he rotates his hips and shoulders, showing some of his back to the opponent. He does this to such an extent that his front foot rotates inward as well. By coiling up in this manner, he generates even more power. His motion has been compared to the former baseball pitcher Luis Tiant, who also used to rotate his back toward the hitter. This coiling and springing produces extra power.

The Back Foot: Sampras positions his back foot past the heel cup of the front foot, which facilitates further turning for more rotational power.

In all of your skills, strive for ease of duplication. Sampras's motion economizes the serve concept. Simply balance on your back foot, lift your arms, and whack the ball.

The Rios Motion

At the 1998 French Open, John McEnroe, as commentator for NBC, relayed a conversation between Marcelo Rios and his coach, Larry Stefanki. Rios told Stefanki that he wanted to serve harder. Stefanki said not to do this, that another top player had tried this and his serve only got worse. Stefanki told Rios to work on his placement and consistency.

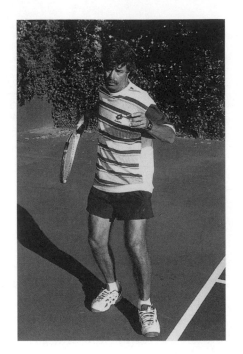

Rios service start, key elements: elbow is pulled back across the stomach.

Rios's motion is a shorter pull across the body start. This is an instance where the goal is to put your elbow in the slot and then unwind. I have gone to this start myself and have had great success. You come across your stomach on the start, keeping your racquet level to the ground. You pull your elbow back, and from this point everything else is the same. The advantage of this shorter motion is there is less to do, thus less can go wrong. Many other players are also using this start, including Carlos Moya, a top ten player who can serve over 125 miles per hour.

Pull-up Ground Strokes

There is a new shot the pros are hitting that is easy to duplicate, pull-up ground strokes, hit at the net when your opponent gives you a low, softer ball. When the shot hit to you has great power, you have no choice but to get low with your body on the plane of the shot and hit a volley or half volley. If the ball is hit softer, though, the better move is to put your brakes on and stop, or even take a step back, let the ball come up, and take a full drive swing. Because the ball is hit softer there is time to calm down and try to control and hit a more aggressive shot. Sampras hits this shot often as he serves and volleys. He recognizes that the return has been weakly hit: instead of charging the volley and hitting off his toes, he pulls up and hits a full shot.

Practice and Mechanics

Practice sessions are used to master your mechanics, a time to work on additions or adjustments to your shots. I call this retooling. When watching the pros play, you may observe that a player has a slightly different start than yours. During practice, you can experiment with what you've seen. You may decide that this change is an improvement and keep the adjustment, or that it does not help your game at all and return to the previous form. Several years ago, after watching Thomas Enqvist, one of the top Swedish players, hit big topspin with an over-the-shoulder finish, I decided to imitate this forehand technique. It took me nine months of work before the shot become automatic. I make minor adjustments to my serve all the time. Although I implemented the Sampras serving style, I still experiment with my back foot's positioning. Until you serve 120 miles per hour, there is room for improvement.

Practice often and you will master your shot mechanics. When you play, you will have confidence in your shots and yourself. Take some inspiration from Todd Woodbridge, one of the top Australian players, who said he derives great joy working on part of his game, then putting it into match play and experiencing the results.

CHAPTER
4

Game-Plan Strategy

Last year at one of the Grand Slams, John McEnroe commented that you must step onto the court with five game plans and be prepared to use all of them. The key to a successful game plan in all sports, tennis included, is to know how you are going to play and how you are going to respond to your opponent. The more you know your next move, the more in control you are. Tennis is often compared to chess because your opponent moves and then you are supposed to react in a controlled countermanner. The keys are knowing how to respond and having confidence in your response system.

Game Plan #1: Serve and Volley; Serve Return and Volley

Serve and Volley

When serving and volleying, you move in toward the net immediately after serving, which requires both a good serve and a good volley. I call this a one-two punch. Even if you manage to return the serve of big server such as Boris Becker or Pete Sampras, they will hurt you badly with the first volley.

The key to success is to decide and commit to this tactic *before* you serve, so you immediately rush the net for the volley. This type of aggressive play usually makes for short points.

Sometimes the act of rushing the net makes you rush your serve. If your service game is off, consider abandoning this plan until your serve becomes forceful again. You should also abandon this strategy if you are not successful with your volley, or if the returner is hitting too many great returns, making your first volley difficult to execute.

Practice

Play full sets in which you commit to the serve and volley, so that you will be comfortable with this tactic in match play.

Defenses

You must return well when facing the serve and volleyer to convince him that there is a low percent of success following the serve into the net. You must pound the ball into and around the volleyer so that he doesn't have enough time to effectively volley. If you can keep the ball low on the return, it will make for a very difficult volley.

Serve Return and Volley

This tactic is employed when facing your opponent's second serve and when facing weak first serves. This is a great way to put pressure on the opponent and shorten the points. Stefan Edberg used this tactic exceedingly well. As with the serve and volley, you must be able to execute a good volley for the combination punch. Decide beforehand to rush the net; after you hit the return, immediately come to the net.

You should abandon this tactic if your opponent's serve is too strong, making it difficult to control your return. You should also abandon this tactic if the opponent is hitting great passing shots.

Practice

Play segments in which one player serves until someone wins ten points; work on coming in to the net after every second serve. The segment play puts less "game" pressure on you. Then start to play entire sets with the same attack focus.

Defenses

Hit your serve deep and hard. It is too difficult to attack and go to the net after a high-quality serve. Another way to counter this tactic is to follow your serve into the net; beat the returner to the net. By attacking the attacker, you cut the time of preparation for the returner on his next shot.

You need to develop effective passing shots and lobs so that when the opponent comes in to the net, your response is cool, nonpanicked, and decisive. You must escape the pressure of the attack through the nine escape holes:

1. Power crosscourt.
2. Dip at the feet crosscourt.
3. At the body with power.
4. At the body dipping at the feet.
5. Power down the line.
6. Dip at the feet down the line.
7. Lob crosscourt.
8. Lob in the middle.
9. Lob down the line.

Each of these may be an equally viable solution. The key to success is to neither panic nor rush when implementing the escape. Pick your solution and execute. The opponent, by coming to the net, is selling pressure, especially in a squeezed time frame. Your response should be to calmly execute your shot; assume that the opponent is just bluffing.

Game Plan #2: Playing Four Zones

The zones are designed to teach you when you should be aggressive and when you should be more patient. Ivan Lendl and Jim Courier both said it was important to learn to stop carrying the burden of the point on every shot. Unfortunately, they never explained the divide between aggressive and patient. Learning the zones will teach this concept.

Zone One

The service square area comprises zone one. If the ball struck by your opponent lands in front of the service line, you are invited to the net. You should step up into the court to hit an approach shot, come off your shot immediately, and go to the net. These days, the pros are mixing the approach-shot location more than ever. In hockey, the shot placement has been labeled; I recently labeled the seven approach shots in tennis.

1. Down the line: makes it easier to bisect the passing angles of the opponent.
2. Up the middle: forces the passer to make her own angles; effective against a speedster who covers the wide shots easily.
3. Crosscourt: best against an opponent's middle-of-the-court shot—however, if you hit it off the severely wide crosscourt shot, you must execute the shot very well; otherwise you open up the down-the-line pass.
4. Angle wide crosscourt: both short and deep are effective locations.
5. Touch approach down the line.
6. Touch approach in the middle.
7. Touch approach crosscourt.

All three touch shots are quite effective if you have been pushing the opponent deep with the other approaches; don't underestimate the value of the surprise element. However, the penalty for a poorly executed touch shot is usually great.

Practice

Both players should stay back at the baseline: player A hits to player B, who gives player A a short ball; player A then steps up to hit one of the seven targeted areas, while player B works on the passing game. Do not play serve and volley in this drill, but when the ball does land in zone one, go to the net.

Defenses

The key to prevent the opponent from attacking you on a short ball is to make sure you hit deeper shots. The keys to hitting deeper are to remember to elongate your drive-through on the finish of your shots. Even when you follow through over your shoulder, you must still drive out first. Furthermore, make sure you are making solid contact with your hit. The more crisply you hit the ball, the deeper it goes. Focus on giving the ball six to ten feet of clearance over the net, because high-clearance balls land deeper.

Zone Two

Zone two covers the eight feet past the service line. When the opponent's ball lands here, you should step up into the court and hit into one of the seven approach-shot areas. The step-up shot should be hit with authority. For pro tennis, this shot has become akin to shooting a basketball free throw. When the ball is hit with less depth, the pro players are stepping up and killing it.

The second form of zone-two hitting is called blitzing, and occurs when your opponent floats the ball back to you. Instead of cooperating by letting the ball bounce, you step up to hit the ball in the air with a full-swinging topspin shot targeted to either side.

Consider the first two-thirds of the court, zones one and two, to be the "attack zones." This will significantly cut down your opponent's footage and the amount of time he has to react to your shots. To be most effective in both zones one and two, you must want to volley and do it well.

Your goals are to reach the net first and to win the point. Some players resist moving to the net because they have no confidence in their volley, and hence put too much pressure on themselves when hitting the step-up shot. Some of the top pros, such as Agassi, Courier, and Seles, do not advance to the net even after hitting a great step-up shot because they aren't comfortable at the net. John McEnroe is critical of Agassi for his failure to follow up his great step-up shots into the net. Quite correctly, McEnroe points out that the volley follow-up would be an easy put-away for Agassi if he were up at the net.

To quickly come off your step-up shot, you must first assume that you are going to hit a very good one. You can't afford to hit the shot, look it over, then analyze its quality before proceeding to the net. Know where you want the ball to go before you hit it, then assume it will go there.

There is a specific dance step required when coming off your shot and going to the net. In the back court, after you hit a ground stroke, you bring your back leg forward so that it is even with the front leg. But after you hit a step-up shot, bring your back leg *past* the front leg. This gives you an automatic run-in step, which will help you get to the net much faster.

On days when you can't serve and volley or serve return and volley, playing the zones still enables you to consider two-thirds of the court as an attack zone. Before I invented the zones in my collaboration with the late Tim Gullikson, people talked about only two zones that were divided by the service line. However, the first zone generally included only the first third of the court, which was considered the attack zone, and the second two-thirds of the court was treated as the stay-back zone. Your net play was basically eliminated on days when you were not able to effectively serve and volley. In the course of the whole match you might receive only six balls landing in the first third of the court. But if you consider two-thirds of the court an invitation to charge the net, you are afforded many more opportunities to be an aggressive net player.

Practice

Use the same drill as for zone one. Player A hits short balls into zone two, and player B steps up to hit the ball, then goes to the net. Play sets where you attack on every ball hit into zone two, going in behind your great shot.

Defenses

The defenses against zone-two attackers are the same as against zone-one attackers. The burden is on you to hit well enough to prevent your shots from becoming invitations to your opponent to pound on. I would place even more focus on your shots' clearance of the net, aiming six to ten feet over it, giving your shot enough air time to land deeper in the court.

Zone Three

This "patience" zone covers most of the rest of court, up to the last six inches before the baseline and a three-foot triangle at the corners. Here you remain a steady hitter, waiting patiently for your opponent's short ball, trying to move your opponent on every shot. Since you are hitting the shot from behind the baseline, you do not follow your ball into the net, due to time limitations; you can't hit a power shot and have it returned with time enough for you to reach the halfway mark to the net. That's why zone three is called the "patience" zone: you must wait for an invitation to come to the net. As long as the opponent's shot is hit deep, in zone three, hit it back with good movement and power, and wait for a short ball.

In this zone you must choose the distance you wish to stand behind the baseline. One of the big trends begun by Agassi is to hit the zone-three shot from close behind the baseline. The closer you are to the baseline, the more you will hit the ball on the rise, which requires better timing. Many players prefer to position themselves farther outside the baseline, which allows more time to sight and react to the opponent's shot; however, this also gives the opponent more time to see and react to your shot.

When Thomas Muster had his great clay-court season in 1995, culminating with a win at the French Open, he said he tried to shorten his distance off the baseline that season. In watching Michael Chang win his semifinal against Sergi Bruguera before losing to Muster in the finals of that tournament, observers noted the big difference in the time frame Chang was given to hit. Bruguera stood eight feet past the baseline, while Muster stood only three feet past, and he would often attack the net after Chang's shorter shots.

Practice

Play ground-stroke drills where you work on recognizing zone-three balls. Work on not forcing the action, staying patient while waiting to be invited to the net. Also play sets to solidify the zones concept and develop a good baseline game.

Defenses

Play more aggressively by getting to the net more often. Either serve and volley more or attack more of the short balls, trying to avoid letting the points last too long. You must also become more patient yourself. Remember that you can always outrally the opponent.

Zone Four

The last few inches of the court and the deep corner triangles are especially challenging.

When the ball is blasted back to the baseline and you are standing close to it, you must hold your territory and flip the shot up. Compact your start, but still drive the ball and continue your follow-through. This flip-up shot is often necessary when hitting the opponent's serve return: you have fallen into the court after your serve and the opponent has cranked the return deep. Since there is no time to retreat, you must bend your knees to the line of the ball and flip it back. A shot the pros are hitting is the fall-back jump shot; the hitter moves backward on the jump, keeping the hit point in front of him, then loops up on the shot so it has some depth. This is a great addition to your game.

If the ball is floated back to the baseline with ten to thirteen feet of clearance over the net, then there is time to retreat; move behind the ball so you can execute the hit shot with your weight transferring forward. For every foot you retreat, you must add another foot of clearance to your shot. By hitting a power high-clearance shot back, you can keep your opponent pinned back and give yourself a little extra time to regain your initial court positioning. If you don't add extra clearance over the net to your shot, your hit will land very short or, worse, go into the net.

When retrieving a ball hit deep to the corner, treat the ball as if it were a regular zone-three ball if you can readily position yourself to hit it. But if you are scrambling for a late hit to your forehand side, hit the shot that Sampras hits, an "out and up" on the same side of your body as you started, because it is extremely difficult to get the full-angle incline of the over-the-shoulder hit on the full run. By following through with a yank-up hit, you can execute the shot with power or loop it up.

When you are scrambling for a late hit to your backhand side, reach back to power-slice the shot. Even if you hit normally with two hands, this is a good time to let go and hit with one, which is what the two-handers at the pro level have added to their game.

Practice

Work on ground-stroke drills wherein you play out the points. Recognize the zone-four ball, and hit the proper response. When playing sets, practice hitting to the different zones and recognizing which zone your opponent's ball lands in and which response is appropriate.

Defenses

The defenses to zone four are the same as for zone three. Again, it is critical that you play more aggressively so that the opponent can't continue hitting your ball so punishingly deep.

Game Plan #3: Baseline Wall

Assume that you own the baseline territory because you are rock-steady. Missing balls that you are able to reach is not allowed. Whatever number of balls your opponent is able to hit, you will hit one more. Martina Hingis, one of the top players in the world, is the foremost proponent of this style. She always has balance, making it difficult to hurt her. She constantly makes her opponents overplay because the opponent has gotten frustrated for receiving no rewards for the good shots. By being steady, Hingis baits the opponent into trying harder and making mistakes.

With confidence in your mechanics, you know your shots will hold up until the cows come home. Many clay-court players use this as their primary strategy, hitting the ball consistently with great spin, speed, and placement. Because they rarely venture to the net, the teasing line we often hear the commentators make is that they only go to the net to shake hands when the match is over.

Use this long-play strategy when you have great confidence in your strokes. When you watch Michael Chang play, observe that this strategy is not the quick one-two punch of the serve and volleyers, but the multi-punch concept of constant blows to the body. Solid ground-stroke baseline hitting wears down the opponent. For this strategy to work, you must be well conditioned, because the matches are going to last longer.

Use this strategy against a wild-hitting opponent. There is no need for you to carry the burden of the point because your opponent hits too many unforced errors. All you want to do is to give him chances to miss.

Abandon this strategy when you're playing someone equally or more steady than you. Against this opponent, you are going nowhere, so you must pick up the offense.

Practice

Work on gaining confidence by improving your consistency work and target shooting. Hit up the middle to see how long the rally can last. Then hit to the corners, working both crosscourt and down-the-line. Aim each stroke and try hitting for at least ten strokes per side per rally before moving to the next aim segment. When you play sets, work on staying back and not missing.

Defenses

The key to stopping the steady baseliner is to reach the net more often. The best tactic is to not engage in long rallies. Be the first one to get to the net, ending the points earlier. But when you are stuck on the baseline, be more patient. Realize that this is going to be a longer match. You must maintain confidence in your ability to outrally this opponent.

Game Plan #4: Hitting Short on Purpose

When you're playing against a person who either hits great passing shots or is a baseline maven, try bringing the opponent in to the net with short shots. In the 1998 Davis Cup deciding match, United States versus Russia, Jim Courier tried to hit Marat Safin off the court, to no avail, losing ten of the first eleven games. Then Courier began to purposefully hit short shots, mostly slices, so as not to give Safin the shots he was so effectively handling. This forced Safin to come in to the net, where he was neither comfortable nor greatly skilled. Courier won the match by adjusting his game plan and broke the Davis Cup tie.

Some players are quite effective in the back court but are afraid of net play. By hitting short, angled balls, you force the opponent out of her comfort zone. Use this plan when you are faced with the steady baseliner, or when your opponent's running ability or net skills are not strong.

Abandon this strategy when the opponent can handle your shots with ease and has a strong net game and a good overhead shot. Many players have tried this strategy against Monica Seles, but it doesn't work: she gets in, says "thanks for the short ball," and proceeds to kill it.

Practice

Develop topspin angle rolls and underspin touch shots so that the ball stays short and moves away from the opponent. A good practice drill is to play minitennis, with both players on the service lines working on touching the ball back and forth. In playing sets, work on hitting both the topspin angle roll-outs and the touch underspin as often as you can.

Defenses

The key to stopping the short-ball hitter is to be able to effectively handle the short shot. First, demonstrate that you have the foot speed required to get to the ball. Second, show that bringing you to the net is an ineffective play because you can coolly respond with one of seven different approach shots to kill the opponent. Prove that you can hit good volleys and overheads, so bringing you in simply sets you up to hit a winner.

Game Plan #5: Down-Pacing

Similar to Game Plan #4, when your offense is not effective and bringing the opponent to the net also fails, then it's time to try down-pacing. In one of tennis's most famous matches, when Arthur Ashe beat Jimmy Connors to win Wimbledon in 1975, he used this tactic. The night before, Ashe met with a few of his friends for dinner. They figured that he would lose if he tried to out-hit Connors, because Connors loved pace. This is true for all players; the opponent's increased pace makes it easier for you to generate pace. The group concurred that Ashe should down-pace his shots. The strategy worked, and Ashe won.

By down-pacing, you can often cause your opponent to overhit as he tries for increased power. Brad Gilbert, a former top ten player on the ATP tour and now Andre Agassi's coach, employed this strategy all the time. He amassed a great record against Boris Becker, one of the game's biggest hitters, by frustrating Becker with his down-paced shots. In the 1996 French Open, Arantxa Sánchez Vicario was losing an early-round match when she switched to heavy down-pacing, and then pulled the match out. The crowd booed her for down-pacing so much, but in the postgame interview she explained that it was the only way she could win against her opponent that day.

Use this tactic when you are faced with a big hitter who thrives on pace. Also use down-pacing when faced with a wild hitter. Give the player softer shots and watch him spray the ball all over the court.

Abandon this strategy when faced with a player who is steady and doesn't mind hitting forever. This opponent will often hit your shot quite effectively, and you may be setting him up to put the ball away.

Practice

Play ground-stroke drill games in which you hit with only two-thirds of your power. Practice your aim segments with two-thirds power. But it's important that you not lose your shot mechanics when you down-pace. When playing sets, use the same strategy: hit for an entire set using two-thirds power.

Defenses

The key is to exhibit great patience. Down-pacers win by watching you lose. Slow down to minimize your errors. You must announce, loud and clear, that you will not miss the down-paced ball. Be prepared to play an extra half hour: this match is going to take a while. Understand that your speed of preparation is not your rhythm of hit. If the ball comes faster, you get ready faster, but still hit at 80 percent power. If the ball comes slower, you get ready slower, and hit at 80 percent power. You don't want to over- or underhit. You still move quickly to prepare, and hit in containment. Don't try to teach this player a lesson by punishing every soft shot that she hits. Shorten each of the zones by two feet, and be prepared for a long day.

CHAPTER 5

Physical Conditioning

You must be prepared to play for a long time, which means you must have the requisite conditioning. When Lendl was number one in the world, he was the best conditioned tennis player. When Courier was number one in the world, *he* was the best conditioned player in the world. Courier is still in great shape. During the 1997 Australian Open, the court temperature topped 120 degrees for three straight days. Courier didn't care how hot it was or how long it took to play the match; he was ready to win. He said that he knows he can concentrate forever because he is in shape to last forever. Many players need to win relatively quickly because they know they can't last long. When you begin to tire, you don't move or concentrate as well. Clearly, in the early stages of the careers of Agassi and Courier, in their matches against each other Courier knew he could beat Agassi if the match went beyond a certain amount of time. Courier had committed to fighting it out as long as necessary.

As you tire, you are able to put forth less body power. Your arm feels as if it has been punched out, so you swing slower, and your legs and feet don't move as well, so you get to fewer shots, losing more points. On your serve, you lose speed because you can't use your legs to spring up. Once your serve becomes a batting-practice pitch, you are broken often.

Many of the top pros have hired conditioning coaches. One of the conditioning coaches I know believes he is the straw that stirs the drink. He watches the tennis coaches come and go with their varying theories on how to perform. However, he believes that unless the player is in top shape, none of the hitting will matter because the player will either not last or will sustain an injury. Until you are in top shape, you will not have the foot speed, endurance, or strength necessary to make you a top competitor. It is not uncommon to play two matches in one day at some tournaments. Thus, you better have the proper conditioning to play every ball. There is no worse way to lose a match that you should have won than being defeated by your own lack of physical conditioning.

Unfortunately, for most players all of the conditioning work required is probably the least favorite part of the sport, but it is necessary for success. Once you have been working on a routine for a while, you will find that the workout becomes an important and enjoyable part of your conditioning, which adds joy to your lifestyle. If you have trouble motivating yourself to do this work, find someone who understands your goals and can motivate you. Often just having a friend join you is enough.

Practice

There are a number of excellent conditioning drills:

One-on-One Sequences: Have one player stand in one corner for the entire point and run the other player around. The runner must get to the ball and hit every shot back to the corner in which his workout partner is standing. Switch jobs.

Two-on-One Sequences: One player runs, hitting all the balls down the line, while two players on the other side of the net hit all the balls crosscourt. Rotate around. In the next cycle, reverse the pattern, having the one player hit crosscourt and the other two players hit down the line.

Ten-Point Servers: Play segments where one player serves until someone wins ten points. This helps you prepare for long service games.

Patience Drills: Play a ground-stroke game in which no one can go for a winner in the first six shots. This will increase your concentration and help you stay in the point during longer rallies.

Fighting Drills: On each and every shot make sure you get to the ball. No rest balls or points. This is very tiring work.

Pitch and Catch: One player stands six feet from the baseline and pitches balls to the other player on the baseline, corner to corner. The chaser must catch the ball, working on foot speed and balance, and throw the ball back to the pitcher, doing this continuously for fifty or more balls. This is a drill Wimbledon champion Pat Cash use to do.

Playing Sets: Occasionally, schedule a set-only play day: play six sets in two split workouts. This drill will prepare you for longer match days.

Sprint Work: End practice by sprinting baseline to baseline thirty times.

Off-Court Conditioning

On-court work must be supplemented by off-court work. Any work you do is important. I have had students greatly improve their movement skills and endurance by taking dance classes. Walking is a great activity. Many people are too intimidated by workout programs because of the time commitment they feel must be made. But remember that the minutes add up. If you can walk for only fifteen minutes per day, that adds up to a lot of minutes at the end of the week.

Footwork

Unfortunately, there is no substitute for running to improve your footwork skills. At some point, you need to work on a road, track, or treadmill, focusing on both endurance and speed. For endurance, practice distance runs. For speed, practice sprint work and hill work. In tennis, you need both skills: endurance to last through the match, and sprint speed to chase the ball. It has been estimated that a player often runs six miles during a match. Stair climbers and slide boards help in this area. To develop faster footwork, jumping rope should be added.

Stretching

Stretching is critical to help loosen, relax, and strengthen the muscles. You should be stretching before and after your workouts. You need to learn how to stretch properly, as you can do damage to your body if you don't stretch correctly. You can watch workout shows on television, buy a book or video, or consult with a knowledgeable friend or trainer.

Strength

Weight work is necessary to develop the strength required for more endurance and power on the court. But it is usually advised that children under the age of fourteen not do any heavy weight work. You need both upper- and lower-body strength to succeed in tennis. Free weights and machine weights are helpful, but you don't need to work with *heavy* weights, as you are trying to build speed as well as strength. You can achieve the necessary gains using ten-pound weights or less. Again, you need to know what you are doing. Either follow a workout show or video, or consult with a friend or trainer who is knowledgeable.

Food Intake

Diet plays an important part in your overall well-being and ability to perform. Just as off-court conditioning is critical to your performance, so is off-court diet, the biggest key to your conditioning and ability to play long matches. Your nutrition must be properly balanced for you to have any chance at successful play.

One of the biggest personal issues is how you are going to fuel yourself for the match. Some players prefer to play on an empty stomach, while others prefer a full one. Find out what works best for you during your practice matches. My doubles partner, Mark Jee, can play both his singles match and our doubles match that follows without having eaten.

In the famous 1996 U.S. Open match against Alex Corretja, Pete Sampras got sick at the end of the match. He said afterward that he learned a lot about fueling himself before and during the match. He felt his inadequate food and drink consumption led to his sickness on the court. The following year at the 1997 Australian Open, one of his matches went five sets in the 120-plus-degree heat, but he survived this one much better, thanks to the lessons learned in the Corretja match.

At many tournaments, food is provided to the players. However, you must be quite careful when you are eating tournament food because you can never be sure how long it has been sitting outside, unrefrigerated, or if it has become contaminated by food-handling personnel. Every once in a while at a pro tournament, a few players struggle with intestinal problems. One of my clients, who is a doctor, insists that all players at any level must prepare their own food. Martina Navratilova, on many occasions, brought a cook along to her major tournaments.

Water

You need to replace fluids as you play. And you cannot rely on the tournament personnel to make water available to you. Recently, a friend of mine forgot to bring water to his match. Although he is quite experienced at tournament play, he simply forgot, and there was no water available. He said that after a short time into the match, all he could think about was how thirsty he was. He lost.

You need to drink water on every changeover. Do not wait until you feel thirsty or dehydrated; drink constantly. If you have cramped up, particularly in the heat, you should drink water after every game.

Other Liquids and Energy Boosters

There are many energy supplements on the market that promise to boost your energy, help your endurance, and aid in recovery faster from a tough workout. Pre-mixed drinks, powders, tablets, bars, and herbs are the current vogue. Experiment with different products to see what works best for you. I take an energy drink on the court when I play matches. I also bring along a caffeinated drink. Although there are studies that show that caffeine may be harmful, I like to drink iced tea during match play. On the changeovers, I take a sip of water, a sip of the energy drink, and a sip of iced tea.

Rest

Tennis is like everything else: at some point lack of rest will burn you out. If you want to play great, you must support yourself with adequate rest.

CHAPTER 6

Mental Conditioning —Attitude, State of Mind, Heart, and Fortitude

Mental conditioning ensures that you have a large enough battery pack to participate for the duration of the match. You must assume that the opponent is going to try to knock your brains out. Your have to learn how to fight, concentrate, and focus—what the professionals refer to as *grinding*. You must be prepared to fight for long points, long games, long sets, and long matches. This is hard mental work that even many top professionals have trouble with. In 1996, Andre Agassi had a mediocre competitive year. Upon close observation, it was easy to see he didn't have his usual fighting spirit. In both the French Open and Wimbledon he exited the tournaments quite early to lesser-ranked players. He would hit big for a few shots, and if the opponent was still around, he would go prematurely for the knockout punch; he was not in a grinding mood. You have to have the tenacity and the patience to play the match. If the opponent wants to go for long rallies, you must always choose to hit one more ball than he does.

71

Attitude

Walk onto the court believing that you deserve to win. Even if you've recently suffered a bad loss or have had a few bad practice sessions, you must still believe in yourself, that all of the work you have put into your game will help you prevail. If you walk onto the court believing you are overmatched, the match is already over; you will be playing for sun-tanning purposes only.

Never underestimate your opponent. You must believe your opponent is capable of defeating you. Boris Becker, the Australian Open's defending champion, lost in the first round in 1997. When reporters spoke to Pete Sampras about this, he said, "All of these guys can play. You must not take any opponent lightly. You must bring your best game to the court for every match if you expect to win. If you think your opponent doesn't merit your full focus and skills, you're going to be defeated." In this tournament, Sampras beat Mark Woodforde 6-1, 6-0, 6-1. Journalists asked him why was he so serious during the sets, especially at 5-0—it appeared that Sampras was playing as if the score were 5-5. Sampras answered that he must play as though the score *were* 5-5 to win. How often have you observed professionals and players at all levels of the game blowing big leads by not maintaining the proper attitude of respect for the opponent?

Maintain your confident attitude in your ability, no matter how well the opponent returns your good shot. When you hit a good to great shot, you would like the opponent to become intimidated and extremely respectful by forgetting her form and movement technique. Unfortunately, sometimes a very high-quality return shot is hit. Don't get baited into trying harder for a greater shot next time, which will lead to overhitting and lots of errors. Likewise, you want to handle your opponent's best shots. Your response must be,

"Nice shot, Opponent. I hope you don't mind if I hit it back equally well." Do not panic on the tough shots.

Similarly, you must not panic when the opponent steps up the pressure by coming to the net. By advancing to the net, your opponent is selling the pressure of time frame: you will have less footage and time to react to the shot. "Rush your response or, better yet, just miss and save everyone some time," he hopes. But your calm response will enable you to execute your passing shot or lob.

One of Pete Sampras's many qualities that he attributes to Tim Gullikson is not quitting during tough matches. If Pete didn't learn this from Tim on the court, he certainly learned it watching Tim fight his battle against cancer. Tim never gave up, hoping until the very end to return as Pete's coach. Pete has played in two of tennis's most memorable matches in the last few years. The first was against Jim Courier in the 1995 Australian Open. It was during this tournament that Tim was diagnosed with cancer. Pete came back from two sets down to make it two sets a piece. A fan yelled out, "Win the fifth set for Tim." All the emotion of the week came out. Pete cried on the court. For a brief moment, Pete's attention was focused on his coach and best friend's condition. But like the champion he is, he regained his composure and focus and returned to the task, prevailing. The other match was the fifth-set tiebreaker against Corretja, in which he saved a match point and won, despite being sick. Winning is an attitude. Not accepting losing is an attitude. Fighting until the last point is over is an attitude.

Practice

Do two-on-one drills (see page 65). This makes one player work extremely hard to win any points, which teaches toughness in handling difficult court situations.

Play sets with lesser opponents, giving them a handicap on every game. This teaches you to battle every point. Play sets from different scores. Start down 4-1, to learn how to battle back. Start up 4-1 to learn how to fight while ahead. Play some sets where the opponent calls all your line shots out to help you get some adversity practice.

State of Mind

During the 1996 U.S. Open, anyone could make Steffi Graf cry by mentioning her father's name. Her father had been in jail for over two years on tax-evasion charges, and his trial was scheduled to start soon. Graf herself had come under investigation for her alleged knowledge of the scheme. A German magazine was reporting that she might also be indicted. But once this tough competitor walked onto the tennis court, she was all business. Her state of mind was not adrift, it was focused. She won the tournament.

At this same tournament, Pete Sampras was also under great emotional stress, greatly upset over the death of Tim Gullikson; much of the off-court commentary was about the loss of Tim. Pete would become teary-eyed whenever anyone mentioned Tim. But on the court, Pete too was all business, and he also won the tournament.

There is no argument that off-court circumstances can make it difficult to fully focus during your match. However, think of bringing to the court a jar into which you put the outside world's concerns. Then step onto the court at full focus, paying absolute attention to the ball. To focus on every shot, go through a loop of six elements to enable you to succeed: read the opponent's shot, react to it, move on balance, use your shot mechanics, use your shot strategy, and reposition for the next shot. You won't perform well if you are not focusing.

Sighting the Ball

Last year, a high school player came to me with the complaint that she and her current coach were upset with her lack of court speed. She was in good shape and a fairly fast runner, but didn't move well on the court. What, she wondered, was her problem? The answer was easy to ascertain. She did not know how to sight and react to the opponent's hit; she had not learned to track the ball to the opponent's racquet.

When the opponent strikes the ball, four variables of that hit are irrevocably determined: direction, depth, speed, and spin. Take a sequence of hit pictures to see the contact quality, the drive quality, and the directional drive of the hit. I call this movement time the *B Stopwatch:* it starts running when the opponent strikes the ball and continues until you hit the ball. Your ability to use the maximum time allocated to chasing the ball greatly increases your chances of reaching it. Once this young lady learned to read the opponent's shots, her court speed improved dramatically.

Andre Agassi did not have a good tennis year in 1996. One could tell that during the last two tournaments of the season, his heart was not into playing. In one match against Mark Woodforde, he regularly did not chase down balls. He hadn't lost his reading ability. He simply, for whatever reason, didn't feel like reacting to what he saw. If your eyes tell your feet where to move, but your feet refuse, you have a major problem.

Move on Balance

When you move, you must move *on balance.* These days, balance means three things: keep your head quiet, with little movement, and no movement during the hit; keep your shoulders on a straight line; and maintain your shoulders over your hips. My business partner, Larry Dodge, one of the top senior players in the country, was watching Agassi a while back and observed how quiet Agassi's head remained, especially when on the run. Larry said of his own movements that occasionally he feels like one of the toys that has its head bobbing all over the place in the back of a car.

Keep your eyes on the ball as long as possible, finishing the shot with your eyes still focused on the hit point. Don't pull your head off the shot to admire your excellent work. Only when you feel the shot has completely left your racquet should you peacefully turn your head toward the flight of the ball. If your shoulders are not resting squarely, your balance is tilted either up or down, which creates difficulty in maintaining a quiet, focused eye on the ball. To center your balance, keep your shoulders over your hips. If you fold down with your waist bent over, it will be difficult to pull your arm up and out toward the opponent. If you lean back or away, you are pulling your body in a direction that will again make it difficult to move your arm forward. Also, if you move your head as though Mike Tyson were punching you, you will not be able to maintain head control when stroking the ball.

Use Your Shot Mechanics and Shot Strategy

When the opponent hits a quality ball, there is no reason to panic. Instead, use your shot mechanics and your shot strategy. At the upper levels in tennis, you must control your side of the net. No matter how good your opponent's shot is, your goal is to hit it back with your learned mechanics and purposeful placement. Many times, when you chase down the ball, it is easy to become engrossed in the chase and forget all about the hit. The entire time you spend running, you should be chanting to yourself, "Got it, got it, hit with purpose."

Reposition After You Hit the Ball

The final point on this loop of six elements is to reposition after you hit the ball. I call this the *A Stopwatch:* it starts after you hit the ball and continues until the opponent strikes his shot. Come off your shot and either advance to the net or retreat behind the baseline. Since you always assume that your shot landed in, you must reposition for the next shot.

One Ball at a Time

To achieve this loop of six elements over and over, you must learn to play each ball singularly and then run the loop of six. In John Feinstein's book *A Season on the Brink,* about Indiana University's basketball program, Bobby Knight is described telling his team that if they were not concentrating and focused, the team was in fact giving away seven points to the opposition. Knight told his players that they were not seven points better than any team, so they would lose the game if they lost concentration. In tennis, the same is true. No player is that much better than the opponent that he can afford to take walkabouts. If you give your opponent three or more free points because you are not fully focused, you are going to lose. The pros refer to the lack of focus as being "loose" or "casual."

Present Tense

Remain focused in the present tense. Although it would be nice to be rewarded with the next point after playing a good one, that doesn't happen. And the reward for a good game or set is not another; you must play each point of each game of each set, one by one. Playing well should instill more confidence to play well, and you must reproduce the excellent level of play over and over.

No Past Tense

When the shot has left your racquet, make no value judgment about its quality. You don't have the time to become aggravated about its poor quality; simply ready yourself for its return. Your opponent doesn't get to catch the ball and claim the point based on your weaker return. He must still return the ball. If you stay focused on the present, you may get a chance at redemption. But if you're still upset about the previous shot, you will miss the incoming ball.

Similarly, if you hit a great shot, you cannot afford to praise yourself during the point. While you are still patting yourself on the back, the return will whiz past you. Recently, many of my students attended the Sybase, an ATP tour event held in San Jose, California. I'm always interested in their observations and comments when watching the pros. They are often astounded at how many great shots are hit off of great shots. The fact that you hit a great shot doesn't mean that your opponent can't return the shot equally well. Part of what makes Sampras (who won this tournament) so tough is his ability to hit great responses to great incoming shots.

No Future Tense

One of the pressure elements that your opponent is trying to sell is concern over the future hit. He would like you to be so worried about his next shot that you don't focus on your present one. The consequence for future worry is a present miss. By clearly focusing on the present ball, you may not have to deal with a future ball.

Furthermore, don't take your eye off the hit too early to admire its greatness. If you do, your incomplete form will cause a miss, so there will be nothing to admire. And don't check out the opponent just before you hit in order to confirm shot selection or continue to target shop. Watch the ball, plan a target, and hit it.

Present Tense After You Miss a Shot

No player can play tennis without missing a shot. When Graf and Seles are winning matches in forty-five minutes 6-0, 6-0, they still miss shots. Somehow, you must bury the last failure and return to the present tense. Past failures shouldn't make you believe that you are incapable of any future success.

There are two methods for dealing with the failure of a shot. One, you can schedule a tantrum for up to fifteen seconds and go nuts on the court. Jimmy Connors used to do this and still does. I too have used this method on more than one occasion. But you must be able to vent and then *stop*. Most players cannot do this, however: they cannot time-frame their anger; the anger stays and more mistakes are made. One mistake becomes three. One bad game becomes three because the player can't get beyond the past failure. Most players would benefit from adopting the Stefan Edberg system: don't say or do anything. If you miss a shot, take a practice swing, and remind yourself how to hit the shot correctly.

Practice

For both drills and sets, learn to stay cool. Play with a radio on to get used to distractions. When I first moved to the Bay Area I used to play in Golden Gate Park. The place is a zoo—people walking and talking, music playing, other players' balls bouncing onto your court during every point. If you could concentrate in this place, you could concentrate anywhere. Play a set and practice scoring drills in which the opponent purposely calls close balls out. Get used to some bad line calls to learn how to maintain your focus. Play someone you do not like. Get used to ignoring the personality on the other side of the net.

Heart and Fortitude

In the summer of 1996 *The Sporting News* carried an article about a baseball player who had undergone career-ending shoulder surgery: Orel Hershiser, a major-league pitcher, had the best definition of heart and fortitude that I have ever heard. Explaining his rehabilitation, he said, "I had the will to go on, even though no progress was being made and none was in sight. I had the will to go on when the pain was so great that the will to quit was far greater than the will to go on. I had the courage to keep on going, to try to win, to recover to the point of playing, even though the risk of losing everything was great."

If you want to win at anything, you must develop a love for that activity. To be successful requires both on- and off-court work. It is easy to shortchange yourself. If you don't develop a love, you will never develop the work ethic necessary to carry you through even reasonably tough times. The growth process doesn't progress along a straight line. At times, you may feel you are regressing, especially when you are adding new elements to your game. The ability to move forward, though, takes heart and fortitude.

Believe in the path you have chosen. There is not a player alive who at some point didn't want to break all of his racquets and never play again. Many players have battled through times when the will to quit was far greater than the will to continue. Heart and fortitude enable a player to advance beyond failures and disappointments. Commit yourself to spending the time and energy necessary to achieve success. You can't fear losing and still maintain your commitment. Be a risk taker—invest in yourself.

One often reads about sports figures who have the heart but not the talent, and others who have the talent but not the heart. The movie *Rudy* is about a young man of limited football talent who through hard work and great heart made the Notre Dame football squad. The fact that he didn't become a star isn't the point. The point is that without heart you will not strive to make yourself the best you can possibly be. The fact that others are better in an endeavor does not belittle your achievement. Also, being among the best in your field should not be viewed as an excuse to relax. Michael Jordan continued to work hard to win more NBA titles; Jerry Rice still works hard to win more NFL titles; and Pete Sampras still works hard to win more Grand Slam titles. Why? All of these athletes have great heart. They define themselves by their performance level. When it counts, they always fully participate.

Far too often, far too many people fall short of their potential. For those with talent but no heart, falling short is inexcusable. Getting by or skating because you are blessed with talent, able to outperform most others at half effort, is a tremendous waste. Don't shortchange yourself. Without developing a love of the endeavor, you will never put in the time, energy, or mental commitment required to be a true success. Less than full effort is failure; less than full effort makes you a loser. There is a famous Vince Lombardi quote: "Around here, we do not do things right some of the time; we do them right all the time." You will never strive to do things right all the time without heart. Doing things at less than full effort is a waste.

Practice

The drills and sets are the same as for attitude and state of mind (see pages 73–74 and 79). Practice playing under adverse conditions to develop some toughness. Play when it is too windy, hot, or cold. Play some drills and sets starting with adverse scoring conditions. Start drill games to 10, with the opponent up 7-0. Start set scores with the opponent up 4-1. Make yourself practice fighting back.

CHAPTER
7

Match Preparation

Part of the challenge of playing tennis is testing your skills in match play. Facing new opponents who have unseen strategies and techniques can be an exhilarating experience, as well as a tremendous opportunity for improvement. Competition makes you stronger, and playing against tougher opponents speeds your growth to the next level. To give yourself every chance of succeeding in competitive play, there are a number of things you can do to make the experience as comfortable as possible. Carrying adequate supplies, equipment, clothing, and food is absolutely necessary for your success.

Bags

When you play a match, there are certain elements that you can't control, such as which opponent you will face. But most elements of the match can be controlled by the equipment you bring in your tennis bag.

Racquets

You need to have a racquet you are comfortable with and trust. New racquets with the latest technology are constantly emerging, and one of the latest additions is the "long body," a longer racquet. While the standard racquet is 27 inches long, the longer racquets range from 27.5 to 29 inches long; one company even makes a 32-inch racquet. This is the racquet industry's third try at this long-body concept. When I was a junior player, Bancroft made a racquet an inch longer; about ten years ago, MatchMate tried it, too. Neither racquet generated much of a market. This time, though, all of the companies are making this model and advertising it extensively, claiming that one or two more inches will give you greater reaching ability and more head speed, since additional head speed can be generated with the extra length.

Michael Chang has been using a long body for three years, and attributes his increased serve success to it. The disadvantage occurs when playing close to the net, because there is more racquet to maneuver quickly. For all shots, a longer racquet may make it more difficult for the player to reach the hit point in order to gain that extra head speed. Because it is longer, it is slower to the hit; but once it gets there, the increased swing arch will generate more power. John McEnroe commented during the 1997 U.S. Open that although the Chang serve was moving faster, it was landing in the service box at a lower percentage rate.

Thomas Muster is one of the pros who have successfully switched to the longer racquet, saying that it gives him more power on the serve and ground strokes, and enables him to hit the ball with more spin. I have observed a fifty-fifty success rate among my students who use the long body. The half that love the racquet are playing much better, and their games have greatly improved. The half that do not like the racquet find it too cumbersome. Muster did say that this racquet requires a longer learning curve for comfort and execution than the standard-length racquet.

The second newest concept in racquet design is the introduction of titanium and hyper-carbon racquets. These new metals are making the racquet substantially lighter. They are being made in standard size and up to two inches longer, and are giving everyone a significant power increase. Due to the lightness of the racquet, it is easier to accelerate the racquet on strokes and serves. These racquets are hot sellers as of this writing, and all my students who have gone to the new metals are playing much better.

The importance of the racquet can't be underestimated. The proper racquet ensures your comfort, both physically and mentally; you will minimize your chance of injury to the arm and shoulder and increase your shot control. Some players need to fine-tune their racquets. Sampras adds lead tape to his racquet head and an overgrip to the grip. I place tape on the bottom of my racquet grip and lead tape on the head. Experiment to see what works best for you. Once you've adjusted the racquet to your liking, you must make precisely the same adjustments to your other racquets.

Although Sampras steps onto the court each match day with six newly strung racquets, two racquets are enough for the average player. Even without any personal adjustments, finding the twin for your racquet can be difficult, since each racquet is different, even when they are the same exact model with the same grip size and weight. As a junior, I would be sent new racquets from Bancroft. I would then go into the local tennis shop to trade these two for two others that felt exactly right. Sometimes, I would have to test a dozen racquets to find the matching twins; I could truly feel their differences. These differences, which occur with all racquets from all manufacturers, can be attributed to a lack of manufacturing quality control. Often at a pro match, you will see the player break a string, then send his coach out to have the racquet restrung during the match. This frame was the player's favorite, and he wants it back as soon as possible.

All of the racquet issues need to be worked out in practice, so that when it is time to play the match, you can focus on the ball and not the equipment.

Stringing

Stringing is another issue that is highly personal in regard to comfort and economy. Factors to consider are the type of string, whether it is gut or a synthetic, and the amount of tension, both of which affect how the ball plays off the strings, as well as the wide range of pricing. Sampras uses an ultra-thin gut string that lasts him two hours at the most. In competition, I use a super-thin synthetic nylon that lasts seven hours. Sampras strings his racquets very tight; John McEnroe strung his very loose. Your style of play, as well as your strength and control, determine the stringing requirements.

Some pros take onto the court different string tensions in their backup racquets because they feel that against certain players and in certain conditions they may want the racquet strung tighter for more power or looser for more control. The wisdom of this escapes me, because the additional variables give the player cause for uncertainty about the equipment. Make yourself comfortable by resolving the stringing issue in practice.

Be aware that temperature also affects the flex of the strings and the liveliness of the balls. The hotter the temperature, the more the strings and the ball are "alive," and the more the ball flies. The colder the temperature, the less flex in the strings and the more "dead" the ball is.

Shoes

Tennis is a sport in which your mobility is as important as any other skill. If your shoes do not fit you properly, you will be distracted by your feet instead of focused on the tennis ball. When Nike wanted to sign Sampras to an endorsement contract, one of the pitches they used was that their shoes would not cause shin splits, from which he had recently suffered. If your feet or ankles hurt, your mobility will be severely limited. In match play, it is always a mistake to wear a brand-new pair of shoes, which often causes blisters that render the player nonfunctional. Use your practice time to break in your shoes so that when you play a match, your feet are comfortable.

In a recent U.S. Open, as Zina Garrison's match was about to begin, her shoe fell apart. She had to run into the locker room to find another player with the same size shoes and borrow them. At the end of Sampras's first-round match in the 1997 Australian Open, his shoe also fell apart. If you are playing in extremely hot weather, it's a good idea to have an extra pair of shoes in your bag, even if only to cool your feet with fresh shoes. In the heat, many players also carry an extra pair of socks for the same cooling purposes.

Shoelaces

It doesn't hurt to have an extra pair of shoelaces in your bag. Even in a new pair of shoes, laces can break.

Towels

On the changeover, it is quite refreshing to towel yourself off. On humid days, you may need to towel off after every point. Don't rely on the tournament personnel to provide you with a towel. On hot and humid days, I use two towels: one I wet constantly with cold water to help cool me down, the other I use to wipe off the sweat.

Wristbands

The purpose of wristbands is to keep the sweat from rolling down your arm into your hand. Some players like these; others do not. Ivan Lendl used to wear a double wristband. If you are going to use them, you need a large supply so that you can change frequently because they become saturated.

Headbands

To keep the sweat from rolling down your forehead or keep your hair out of your eyes, a headband is a must. Because they become wet during the match, they need to be changed often, so put a fair supply in your bag. Agassi used to wear a bandanna on his head, similar to a pirate. The thin material gets wet and is rendered useless quite quickly, so you need a good supply if you choose to wear them.

Overgrips

Many players like to use overwraps on their grips. These are designed to absorb sweat and make the grip softer. They are not meant to last long, so you need a supply of replacements. Pete Sampras changes his overgrip often during a match. On changeovers, he quickly rewraps a new one.

Band-Aids and Adhesive Tape

Always carry a box of Band-Aids and adhesive tape in your bag for those unexpected blisters, cuts, and scrapes. Because the skin on my hand is sensitive to cold and dry weather, I often have skin splits that I must tape, covering the skin problem and enabling me to continue playing.

Lead Tape

Some players add small pieces of lead tape to their racquet to make it heavier. Sampras, Todd Martin, and many other professionals place lead tape all over their racquets. If you use lead tape, be sure to carry a replacement roll in your bag. During play, some tape may get scraped off or become unfastened.

Liquids

You must bring the liquids that you want to drink. From your water to your energy drink, make sure you're comfortable. Never rely on the tournament to have these supplies for you.

Tennis Balls

Always carry extra balls for practice sessions. Before your match, you should do some hitting. Sometimes, the tournament site will have extra courts available for practice. Prematch warm-up is great preparation. Don't rely on others to have tennis balls; bring your own to take advantage of this opportunity.

Clothes Bag

Many of the pros carry two bags onto the court: the first is filled with equipment, the second with apparel—extra shirts and a change of clothes for this match and others that may be played on the same day. Even at the pro level, at least three times a year, a tournament becomes backed up due to rain, requiring the pros to play two matches in one day.

It is essential that you have a fresh set of clothes for more matches that day. And during a match, many men change to a dry shirt at regular intervals. Some tournaments are now making arrangements to provide a space for the women to change apparel courtside. A wet shirt weighs you down. Changing the shirt makes you feel more comfortable, so bring along enough extra clothes to last you throughout the day.

Apparel

As with your shoes, proper-fitting clothes are a must. Clothes that are too small, too big, rubbing you uncomfortably, or ones with labels that scratch will distract you from your game. In practice, learn what you want to wear.

After you have completed your match play, you will probably want to shower and freshen up. Most tournament sites will have shower facilities, so you'll need a postmatch change of clothes. Pack some comfortable after-match wear, including a pair of dry shoes. You'll also need shower towels and a plastic bag in which to put your damp clothes. And don't forget soap, shampoo, and a hair dryer, if needed. Come to the match prepared to play and also to clean up afterward.

Develop a checklist of all of the above things that you wish to have in your bag, and make sure that everything you want to bring to the match is included. Do this the night before your match.

CHAPTER
8

At the Match

The Court Surface

For outdoor play, the main surfaces are clay, grass, and hard court. Indoor surfaces are clay, hard, and carpet, which plays like grass. The indoor surfaces play exactly as the outdoor.

Clay

In Europe, red clay is used for most surfaces. This surface plays slow because its granulation grabs the ball and slows down its flight path. The surface is also slippery; stopping on a dime is not possible. Clay players need to learn how to slide into shots and how to reposition without falling on their faces.

In the United States, although there is some red clay, most clay is a granulate green surface, Har-Tru, which is similar to the red clay in that it plays slow, just not *as* slow. The player again needs to learn how to control his body on the slippery surface.

Both types of clay courts are affected by weather. The wetter they become, the slower they play; the drier, the faster. Clay surfaces greatly favor the baseline player with a lot of patience. Many great players with a power game have come to the French Open and played on red clay, only to fail time and again. John McEnroe, Stefan Edberg, Boris Becker, and, as of this writing, Pete Sampras, the best serve-and-volley players over the last fifteen years, have never won the French Open.

Grass

Grass is found less and less mainly due to the difficulty in maintaining it. A few clubs in the United States still have this surface, and even the pro game has a small grass-court season, with Wimbledon being the highlight. This surface does not grab the ball; thus it stays low and skids. This greatly favors the serve and volleyer. Points played on grass usually last just a few shots.

Hard Courts

Hard courts of varying speeds are made from an asphalt or rubber composition. In the Bay Area, one of the latest vogues in court construction is the rubberized surface, which has a little more spring in it, so it protects the body slightly. Sand is added to the paint surface of a hard court, and the more sand added, the slower the play. As time goes on, the surface wears down and the court speeds up. You may play at a facility where the courts have different speeds, because all the courts aren't resurfaced at the same time. A medium-speed hard court allows all styles of play to have a sporting chance. The court has enough speed to reward a serve-and-volley-type player, but it is slow enough to also let a ground-stroke game prevail. In the United States most courts are of this surface, and the pros play an extensive summer North American hard-court season ending at the U.S. Open.

Playing the Surfaces

In many cases you will never be forced into learning how to make adjustments to the various types of surfaces because your area has only one type of court. Most of the East Coast has only Har-Tru courts, and most of the rest of the country only has hard courts. Some clubs do have a mixture of surfaces, which is to your benefit because you can practice the necessary adjustments. However, it is usually only when you travel on vacation or for tournaments that you must deal with the variety of surfaces.

Part of the fun and growth of your game is to try to expose yourself to the different surfaces and to learn to adjust your style and game plans. With exposure to the various surfaces you may find that you dislike a surface so much that you wish to avoid playing on it, or you may also find it such a challenge that you wish to practice on it more until you have a comfortable mastery. Even the pros, who have some mandatory tournament-participation rules, often limit their play on a certain surface that doesn't favor their games.

Today's Conditions

Sun

At some point the sun causes problems for all players. At certain times of the day the sun is in the flight path of your service toss. The solutions are: learn to turn your head away from the sun, still squinting at the ball; in extreme cases you may have to move your toss position; and wear a hat and/or sunglasses. On courts that face east and west instead of the traditional north and south, the sun will be so low early and late in the day that it will affect you. Besides the above-mentioned solutions, you can use your nonhitting hand as a sunshield.

Shadows

Shadow conditions are equal, and the difficult light is the same for both players. However, some players see better in the dark. The better your eyesight in general, the less the shadows will affect you. Many players truly lose the flight path of the ball as it flows through the different light patterns. There are some sunglasses that enhance the color of the ball, making it easier to see. In practice, play matches with shadow light so you can get more used to the changing light pattern.

Lights

Even if you play pro tennis, stadium lighting is not nearly as optimal as natural sunlight. One year when the Oakland A's baseball team was particularly success-ful, they hit with a substantially higher average during their day games than at night. These are among the best athletes in the world, and even they don't function as well in diminished light. At the club level, if you are lucky you may have four light standards per side, but usually there are two. The only consolation is that the lighting is diminished for both players. Even with great lights overhead, it is difficult to follow a ball out of a black sky. At the U.S. Open, where one or two matches are featured per night, you can clearly see the players' initial struggles to get used to the light.

If you are having difficulty with the lights, move your court position back a few feet to give you extra time to see the ball. Adjust your game plan to make your opponent hit more balls in the tough light.

Wind

There is no bigger external factor on the court than wind because it often takes no set direction or speed. The wind is called the great equalizer of the players: the better player doesn't need his shots to be aided by extra movement, and the lesser player gets a bonus beyond his skills because the wind moves the ball better than he ever could. Serving becomes more balanced, as the bigger server has his serve diminished by the wind, and the lesser server's serve was weak to begin with. You may be forced into lowering your toss so the wind can't affect it as much. This guarantees less body involvement from you, thus a weaker serve. On a windy day you should try to get to the net more often, hitting the ball at an earlier time in the flight path so the wind does not make it dance around as much. Never aim a shot out of the court assuming that the wind will blow it in; the wind always seems to die down at that moment. Furthermore, on your aimed shots, give yourself an increased margin in case the wind gusts.

Your attitude about the wind will greatly affect your game. I tell my players to think of a windy day as a mental-toughness day. You must look at the opponent and understand that if this player should not have beaten you under normal conditions, you must rise above the bad conditions and forbid this player to beat you simply because it is windy.

Temperature

This affects what you need to wear, your fluid replacement, and the tennis ball's liveliness. If you are too cold or too hot on the court, your main focus will be on your discomfort rather than on the match. On match day you should be prepared and dress for the weather. Depending on the time of year, the type of day, or the time of day, the conditions can vary greatly. Your success in dealing with the changes will greatly affect the match outcome.

In the cold you must spend an extra amount of time warming up before a match, because it's much easier to pull a muscle. You need extra layers of clothing, including compression tights, warm-up outfits that you can move in, turtlenecks, and a hat to keep your head warm. When clothes are layered you can peel off some as you get warm. Use a leg warmer on your racquet hand that covers the racquet *and* your hand, allowing you to maintain the hand on the grip and still stay warm. You still need to replace fluids.

The balls are also affected by the cold—they don't bounce as much. Often it feels as though you are hitting shot puts rather than tennis balls, so you must bend your knees more when the ball isn't going to rise as much.

When it's hot, it's critical that you wear lightweight and light-colored clothes. You also may need to change your outfit often, since a wet shirt becomes a weight to lug around. Fluid replacement is critical on hot days to avoid cramping. Wear a white hat, and if the brim bothers you, cut it off. Rod Laver used to put a wet cabbage leaf under his hat to stay cool. All of these make a great difference in the amount of heat that hits your head. There are other products to keep you cool, including a cooling kerchief for your neck and wetting your wristbands. Keep a cool, wet towel to wipe yourself down on the game changes. The balls become much more lively in the heat, bouncing more and traveling farther. You need to impart a fraction more spin on the ball to keep it in.

Going to the Match

In all tournaments, you are responsible for finding out what time you are scheduled to play. In most cases, when you enter a tournament, if you send a self-enclosed, stamped postcard or envelope, the tournament director will send you your time of play. If you have not received a card, it is still your responsibility to check in at the tournament on time—phone the tournament desk to find out your starting time. Tournaments have mandatory default-time rules: five minutes late costs you one game, ten minutes late costs you two games, and fifteen minutes late costs you the match.

A few years ago John McEnroe was defaulted out of the U.S. Open doubles for being late. He had left in plenty of time to reach the arena, but ended up stuck in traffic. Even though he had a cellular phone and called the tournament to advise them of his plight, he was defaulted. The U.S. Open officials told McEnroe, who at the time was still highly ranked, that rules were rules, and no exceptions would be made.

Prematch Rituals

Playing a tournament or a team match places much greater stress on the player. Playing a team match places pressure on you from not only the opponents, but from your teammates as well, as they need your win. It's not unusual to feel a little nervous as you go to play. The best way to have your emotions and mental state ready to play is to have a constant set of prematch rituals for *all* circumstances, to help you feel that each match is very much like the last.

Hitting

You need to hit before you play your match to reach a state of preparedness on all your shots. You should hit each shot enough times that you feel confident about it. Luke Jensen has commented that Agassi warms up until he feels confident about his down-the-line backhand—once that shot is grooved, he knows he's ready.

To prevent injury to your arm, it is critical that you adequately warm up your shoulder, especially in cooler weather. In football, the coaches flip out if the starting quarterback is hurt and the backup must go in without having adequate practice throws. In baseball, if the pitcher becomes injured, a relief pitcher is allowed unlimited warm-up time to ensure that his shoulder is loose.

Coaching Time

If you are fortunate enough to have your coach come to a match, spend a few minutes reviewing your basic game plan. If your coach isn't able to attend, then you should go over the game plan during your last lesson. If you have played your opponent before, you may be able to design a better start plan for this round, or you may be able to discuss an opponent that you have been able to scout.

Quiet Time

Before a match starts it's important that you spend some time preparing yourself mentally for the battle ahead. You should be going over your game plans and defenses, focusing on how you plan to play. One former pro player, John Wilkerson, used to sit by himself and stare at the tennis ball to help him focus. Phil Jackson, the former Chicago Bulls basketball coach, wanted his players to do something similar: take a ball into a quiet corner and visualize how they planned to play. Of all the reasons to lose a match, not getting your head into the match is probably the least acceptable. You need to understand what you are going out to do, focus on it, and then do it. You must clear your mind of any thoughts other than what is required to achieve success.

Stretching

Before and after you play stretching is mandatory. Part of your warm-up routine must include an all-inclusive stretching program. Stretching not only helps your body to prepare for the physical workout, it also helps your mind focus on the match. Stretching helps keep your muscles loose and limber, which prevents the dreaded sports injuries.

Preparing to Win

As you step onto the court to play a match, you must believe that you are going to win, no matter who you play. After all of the practice and work you have put into your game, you must believe in yourself. In most cases, you are playing tier tennis, so you will be either a little better or a little worse than your opponent. Having a winner's attitude is critical for success. Even if you know your opponent is supposedly better, remember that everyone has an off day, and that on any given day, anyone can beat anyone else.

If your team has six positions, don't complain if you are playing the one or two spot (position), stepping onto the court with the attitude that you would have a chance of winning if you weren't playing so high. Likewise don't complain that you are playing the five or six spot and the match is not worthy of your participation. In your doubles matches, don't complain about the selection of your partner, having the attitude that you would win if only Joan were your partner instead of Sue.

Schedule of the Match

Often players are squeezing their league or tournament matches into their busy days. But if you've scheduled another appointment three hours after a match, you will be focused on the time frame of the match instead of winning it. As you hurry your match along, you're going to play much worse than usual with each glance at your watch. And defaulting because you don't have time to finish a third set is a foolish way to lose the match.

If you enter a tournament that has matches scheduled Monday through Friday, but you can't play on the last two days, you are obviously limiting your incentive to win. Why win Wednesday when you can't play Thursday? In fact, why win at all, because you won't be able to finish the tournament? This type of a time squeeze doesn't help your performance, nor is it fair to your opponents.

Prepare Your Mind

There is a tendency for players to look at themselves and, at times, disbelieve their abilities and learned skills. Even the number one player in the world loses occasionally and has doubts. You must never, not for one moment, ever consider yourself a loser. You must never believe that your game is not good. While it's possible to win league matches most of the time, it is impossible to win all of them all of the time. In tournaments, all but the winner eventually lose. If you have lost your last few matches, you might develop a diminished attitude. But instead of harping on the losses, you should go back to the practice court to address the shortcomings that led to the losses.

Today's Opponent

An Unknown Opponent

Try to gain some information about an unknown opponent by asking other players. Even at the pro level there are new faces all the time. The first time Sampras played Albert Costa, he was a qualifier at the French Open. Costa gave Pete a very tough match, as Pete had no idea of how Costa played or of what he was capable.

A few years ago, I played a match against a nationally ranked player who I had never seen play. But one of my friends was able to give me a complete scouting report that greatly helped my strategy. Because of the opponent's serving style, I made a slight adjustment inward to compensate for his very spinning but short serve. Without the report, it would have taken me a game or two to make the required adjustments. But with it, I started out the match with an adjusted position and broke serve immediately.

Ranked Above You

This is a free match. You have nothing to lose, since in theory you are *supposed* to lose. Your ranking can't be hurt because the player is already ranked above you, and if you win, you increase your ranking. It is easier to play loose because the higher-ranked player can only defend, so he should be the one feeling all the pressure. Thus, it is also easier to commit to playing with every weapon you know.

The higher-ranked player usually has a better game and hits a better shot. Since he is providing good rhythm and consistency of hit, you may have an easier time against this opponent, up to the point that you can handle his balls. The better incoming shots may make it easier for you to focus more intently.

Ranked Below You

This is the tougher match because you are defending your position. It is easier to be tight and concerned when you have to win just to maintain the status quo. Due to the added pressure, many players will encounter more difficulty finding their rhythm and maintaining a consistency of hit against lesser opponents who don't generate the pace the better player prefers. Particularly on the service motion, the superior player often conservatively down-paces the second serve, feeling there is no penalty for hitting a weaker shot to a weaker opponent. The big catch is that the more one practices being conservative, the more difficult it is to suddenly become aggressive.

Someone Who Has Beaten You

You Got Killed Before

You've worked on the elements of your game that were responsible for the previous loss, and you feel better about your chances this time. Even if you realistically feel that the gap between you and the opponent is too great, make it your goal to stay on the court longer, as the fastest path to becoming a better player is playing matches like this. Learn as much from this match as you can. Normally, this opponent would never ask you to play, so enjoy the challenge and the hitting as best you can.

You Stayed Close but Lost the Last Match

Believe that this time you can win, as you have worked on a few elements of your game that can turn the match this time. In any close match, playing slightly better and winning a few more points could have changed the results. Playing the person again gives you the advantage of a greater awareness of the opponent's style. After playing someone three or four times, you should come to know the opponent's game quite well, and this time you can turn the corner. Step onto the court believing that today is your day to win.

Someone You've Beaten

You Won Easily Before

Assume that the match will be much tougher this time, that your opponent has worked very hard on her game and has improved. Assume this opponent was having a bad day the last time and that it will not happen again. In other words, play respectfully, not taking this opponent too lightly, for the day you do is the day you will lose. Walk onto the court with the attitude that you are facing a great player.

You Barely Won the Last Match

Although the closeness of the match could have been caused by a slight down-playing on your part, this is a match in which you must be extremely focused. This opponent is close to your talent level. Often a few points will determine this match, so try to play your best and focus on prevailing again.

CHAPTER
9

Key Match Concepts

Play Today's Match

When you play a tournament, it's easy to look ahead in the draw and start to worry about the next match. The surest way to lose today's match is to forget to focus on this particular opponent. Sampras has a tendency to barely get by the early rounds, as if he's saving himself for later. Jim Courier, who beat Sampras in the first round of the 1997 Italian Open, said, "It is better to play Pete in the early rounds of any tournament because he gets tougher as the tournament progresses." You can't play later in the tournament unless you win earlier.

The Importance of Each Point

In a match your goal is to build pressure into each point of each game, in each set, as early as possible. If you're constantly winning the deuce point and can convert the ad point to the win column, you're transferring the pressure from the ad to the deuce point. The opponent can no longer lose the deuce point, because the penalty is losing the next point and thus the game. As this pattern continues, your confidence grows in winning this two-point package.

Unfortunately, the opposite is also true. If you win the deuce point but are constantly failing to win the ad point, the opponent feels no pressure, because you can't convert it for the win. Furthermore, you won't care that you win the deuce point, and your failure to convert it will destroy your confidence in finishing off games.

If you can build the pressure back to the deuce point, your next goal is to build the pressure back all the way to the beginning of the game. If you get a nose ahead at the 30-15 point or the first one or two points of the game and you run with the game, you've added tremendous pressure.

Game Points

It's critical for your mental welfare that you have a high conversion rate of game points to games won. One of the first pros I worked with told me that he liked to experiment at 40-love, feeling that if he lost a point he still had two more game points. Unless you are clearly superior to your opponent, this is a risky tactic. Finish the game now.

Your opponent has two choices when you have game point: he can give up, which would be very nice; or, faced with no more margin for error, he can step it up big-time and fight like crazy to take the game from you. You must expect the latter, and be ready for a tough battle.

Game Points Against You

Take it one point at a time and battle back. The more game points that you save, the more you will gain in competitive toughness and confidence, and the more you will pressure the opponent. Match commentators used to say when Boris Becker was serving and down love-40 that he was really "even," because he could simply hit three big service winners to tie the score.

Rebreaking

The easiest time to break the opponent is right after the opponent has broken you. There is a tendency to let down after a break of serve, as the urgency of your hold is not quite so great. Furthermore, often the opponent is so happy she got the break that she is not fully focused during the next game.

Your goal after achieving a service break is to avoid this letdown. Consolidate your service break by holding serve yourself. If you frequently have your serve broken after you break, there is no mental boost, because all this does is keep you even.

Set Points

Again, the opponent has two choices: give up or get tough. You must assume the opponent will play tougher. Play big points as aggressively as you played those that brought you to this point. If you have been serving and volleying, continue doing it. If you haven't been serving and volleying, don't start now, as trying to play bigger than your style allows will get you in trouble. If you have been returning big, keep it up.

Don't go into the prayer mode, hoping the opponent will give you the set, and don't play tentatively. Tell yourself that if you ever plan on playing a good point in your life, this is the time to do it.

Set Points You Don't Get

If you fail to convert a set point, it is important that you don't berate yourself. If one set point escapes, get others until you win the set. On occasion a set will slip by because of the failure to convert the set point. Stay tough to fight the rest of the match. Last year at a pro tournament, one of the young women I used to work with had set points escape her in the first set, which she lost. For the entire next set, she was moaning about the lost opportunities of the first set, and she got rolled in the second set. Once a point is over, it is over. Forget about it, and be determined not to let the next set slip by.

Match Points

Once you're positioned one point away from winning the match, you must have as close to a 100 percent conversion rate as possible. If you play enough matches, one or two may escape you. However, if you're on the brink of winning, it is mandatory that you step up your game. Like game and set points, the opponent either gives up or comes at you with all he has left. Count on the latter.

Often at match point, the opponent gets loose and starts to shoot for the moon, becoming a superman. Since a match point is simply one more set point, play it aggressively in the style of play that brought you to this point. Tell yourself that all of your training has brought you here, and you deserve to win because you have learned to win.

Match Points That Slip Away

The match is not over if you fail to convert a match point. If one match point slips from your grasp, get another, and another until you succeed. You have to tell yourself to fight on. In the 1997 Wimbledon quarter-finals, Sampras had match points in the third set against Petr Korda. He played them big, but Korda still prevailed, winning that set. In the postmatch press conference, Sampras said it would have been easy to dwell on the fact that he could have been in the locker room with the win. However, he knew he couldn't do that. Instead, he had to regroup and play tougher, which he did, winning in five sets. If you act like a balloon with a puncture in it, you will lose the match.

Losing a match in which you had match points is a tough situation from which to recover. Look at the positive side, which is that you played well enough to bring yourself to the brink of victory, and take solace from that.

Don't Make Excuses

Recently, I asked one of my top 3.5 players when she was going to start playing to her ability during her matches. Half in jest, she told me, "When I run out of excuses." There are many reasons you could have won today, but, you didn't because . . . Be responsible for yourself during the match, and you will not have to worry about why you did not win.

You Can't Be the Excuse

No Overreactions

Every player misses shots, including some on important points. When an error occurs, treat it as an aberration; it will not happen again for quite some time. If after a miss you act as though you forgot to bring that shot to the match, the match is over. You can't let one shot make you believe that your game came with only fifty good shots and now that you've reached fifty-one you're doomed. You must have enough confidence in yourself that you can withstand some mistakes and not let a few become a runaway pile of errors.

The form doesn't fail you; you fail the form. The video of your form must be permanently etched on your brain's hard drive. If you missed a shot, you did not use the correct form. Tennis balls are stupid. They show no respect if you don't use your good mechanics, even if you are a top player. The checklist of what could be wrong is long, and by the time you've gone through the list the match will have long been over. So rather than focus on what's wrong, focus on making the shot right again. Walk away for a second, close your eyes, and run the video of the shot being hit correctly.

A big element to not overreacting is to go with the reality of the day, using more of what is working best. Don't force the action. If you are a little off, don't try to make the shots so great: settle for good, giving yourself a wider margin for error. You can't keep missing a shot repetitively. I don't care who you are, or how mentally tough you are, eventually, missing will get to you and bring you down.

Your body language is important. If you mope around the court and act as if the world is collapsing around you, eventually you're going to buy into that. You must maintain positive body language. Commentators constantly remark how Stefan Edberg and Pete Sampras worked very hard on not moping on the court when the match wasn't going as planned. If you start to act depressed and defeated, a smart competitor will sense this and become more inspired. When you act down and out, you are announcing to the opponent that he is getting to you, which will pump him up. Learn how to handle the ebb and flow of the match and your emotions so that you act steadily throughout.

Don't Beat Yourself Up on the Opponent's Good Shots

Learn to differentiate between your errors and the opponent's good shots. When the opponent hits a good shot, either say nothing or acknowledge the good shot. When you say "good shot," it is not overrespect, just a quick cleansing of the shot. If you beat yourself up after your opponent hits a good shot, you're too hard on yourself, making it almost impossible to prevail.

Don't Choke

Choking happens when you make yourself a nervous wreck and can no longer perform. Your arms and legs become heavy, impairing your ability to move. One of the terms for choking is called "having the elbow," which means your arm is so tight that you can't move your elbow to hit. It is always tougher to play when you feel that you're the defender, having a great deal to lose if you don't win. The key is to not care who the opponent is. Just play the ball, one point at a time. Don't play not to lose. Use your form and game plan, stay loose, and try to have a good time. Shake out your limbs and move between points to relax.

Some players choke when a win is imminent. Why would anyone be afraid of winning? Some players, as they near the finish line, tense up. Jana Novotna had Steffi Graf dead in the Wimbledon final a few years back at 4-1 in the third set. At that point she totally collapsed. Greg Norman, the fine Australian golfer, has blown final-day leads on many occasions, but none greater than a nine-stroke lead on the final day of the Masters. It is often said that the toughest service hold is when you are serving for the match. As victory approaches, continue playing as you have been, using your mechanics and game plan, staying loose, and the results will flow. You need to believe that all your hard work has brought you to the deserved victory. There is nothing to fear.

Will Yourself to Win

Don't accept losing. On days when the match isn't going as well as you like, knowing that you have heart and fortitude can carry you through. The better you become at fighting tough matches, the more this becomes part of who you are, and your image of yourself as a competitor skyrockets. There will be days when your physical skills may be diminished, but you will always feel good after a match if you know that you fought your hardest throughout. There are many players who can't fight when they're behind—it's as if they have fits because they can't win easily. When you are hot you should win. And it's when you are not at your best that developing the ability to fight through to win is what makes you a great competitor.

The Opponent Can't Be the Excuse

One of the biggest excuses for losing a match is that you didn't like the play style of the opponent. This is why you must master your defenses to different games. You don't get to vote on the style the opponent plays. You must deal with it.

The Opponent Acted Wrong

One of the most common excuses for losing is that the opponent's conduct didn't meet your expectations. Nine times out of ten, the opponent's conduct has nothing to do with you—from the way she bounces the ball and pauses between points to the way she looks at you or ties her shoes should have nothing to do with you. Don't take the activities personally.

In a 1997 match Jeff Tarango played Thomas Muster and mimicked him throughout the match. Tarango said he felt he couldn't beat Muster with his physical game, so he tried to disrupt his mental one. When you are confronted with this type of sportsmanship (or lack thereof), just laugh it off. You should take the compliment that the opponent is giving you: he knows he can't beat you fair and square, so he is resorting to gamesmanship. Ignore the antics.

Line Calls Can't Be the Excuse

Balls touching any part of the line at any and every point in the match are good. Usually the better the player, the better his line calls—experience on the court gives players a greater sense of where the ball has landed. *Parallax* is the term given to the common visual distortion that from a distance there is a visual push outward, giving the impression of good shots being out. If you are standing right on the line, believe your eyes. If you are standing at the net and turn to see a ball land three inches or less *outside* the line, it actually landed *inside* the court, so it must be called good. On a clay or Har-Tru surface, you can check the mark the ball leaves; on all hard-court surfaces, in fact, you should be able to do the same thing. By and large, if you call lines liberally, your opponent will reciprocate. Likewise, if you call close balls out all the time, expect close calls to go against you. Your opponent is out to beat you; don't give him an extra incentive to beat you because he thinks you're making incorrect line calls.

Disputing Line Calls

If Your Opponent Is Challenging Your Calls

No one makes calls perfectly every time. If you're standing right on top of the line and are sure of your call, stand firm. But if the ball landed a distance away from you, and the opponent is standing on the line of the call, her view is superior to yours, and more likely to be correct. If you want to play a low-tension match, reverse your call.

But if the opponent is constantly challenging your calls, you should ask your team captain or tournament director for help in calling the lines.

If You Are Challenging Your Opponent's Calls

You should not tolerate poor line calls: if the lines are floating, you'll fear hitting the ball too close to the line. Missing a close call can happen. But once the disputed calls number three, you and the opponent are seeing things differently. Go to the net and politely tell the opponent you feel the need to have help calling the lines.

Matches with a One-Chair Umpire

On clay or Har-Tru courts, you can stop play and request that the umpire come and inspect the mark. On all other surfaces, there is very little you can do to argue the umpire's call. Often, the chair will tell the players to make all the calls, with the chair only correcting errors.

Matches with Umpire and Full Linespeople

Again, on the soft courts, stop play and request that the chair umpire step down to look at a mark. If you feel that a particular linesperson is making errors, you can ask the chair umpire to remove that official, but it will probably not happen.

Being a Great Sport

On occasion in matches with umpires or linespeople, you will see a player make the correction himself. The chair umpire had called it out, but the player gives the opponent the point because he knows the chair was wrong. The reason you don't see this done more often is that the players are told not to do this because the chair umpire has the final word. Early in his career, John McEnroe gave points away by correcting the chair, and was told not to do this by fellow players—in no other sport does the player correct the umpire.

Disputes Can't Be the Excuse

Double Bounces

One area of dispute on the court occurs when one side sees a double bounce, called a "not-up" shot. When the ball bounces twice on the hitter's side, the player is responsible for calling this on himself. If there is a chair umpire, she is supposed to call this. At times, it's quite obvious; other times, though, the second bounce and contact are extremely close. When Agassi was number one, he played a match in which he argued that the shot he'd just made was hit before the second bounce; the chair umpire said no, the ball bounced twice. Television replay showed Agassi was wrong—even the top players at times can't tell when the shot was hit. I instruct all my students to play through the opponent's possible not-up shot and argue it later. Don't waste a point by catching the ball and disputing whether the shot was good. In a nonumpired match, someone is going to have to give in.

Ball Hits Player on the Fly

The point is automatically lost, even if the player hit was out of the court or was trying to escape from the ball. As with the double bounce, the player who is hit must confess, and the point is lost. Sometimes it's clear what happened. One of my top juniors lost a match when on match point for the opponent, in a third-set tiebreaker, the ball hit my student's foot, four feet outside the court. Both players had no trouble seeing this. Goran Ivanisevic played a tiebreaker recently in which the opponent hit the ball long. Ivanisevic tried to escape it and thought he had, but the umpire ruled the ball hit his foot. Goran argued that the ball had bounced first, but replay showed the umpire was right.

External Factors Can't Be the Excuse

Disregard what the crowd does or says. Players often get spoiled and insist on ideal playing conditions. When any noise or movement outside the court occurs, they become unreasonably disturbed. John McEnroe was the worst offender in this regard—he could spot a fan moving a hundred feet away. When you are focused on the match at hand, bombs should be able to drop ten feet away and you wouldn't hear or see them. When you are looking around, you are not concentrating. A player once threatened to stuff a ball down a fan's throat because the fan was cheering too much for his opponent. You can't let the crowd unravel you.

Mark Philippoussis, a top pro, said when he first started playing the crowd would get excited about a powerful shot he hit, so he would then try to hit the next one even harder to please the crowd. This often led to him being extremely wild. The crowd is not the opponent and has nothing to do with the match.

Family and Coaches Attending Your Match

It's nice to have someone in your corner cheering you on, which can inspire you to stay focused and maintain the fight. However, some players look to the family or the coach on every point, needing constant reassurance that life is great. These spectators must also be careful to not be negative in their reactions to the match, or the player will feel greater pressure. Often the player is more concerned with these interactions than the match. While it is nice that there is someone trying to keep you pumped up, don't be so dependent and frail.

If the family member or coach yells, "Come on, Al, big point. Let's get that break point," you may well receive a point penalty for being coached. As with all penalty points, accumulate three and you are out of the match. Matches have been defaulted due to illegal coaching.

A good use of the friend in the stand is to have this person chart or film the match.

The Match

Entering the Court

As you step onto the court with your match bags, limit your conversation with the opponent to stay focused on the job at hand. The pros do not make small talk as they walk on the court together. The time to be friendly is after the match, not before.

Never ask the opponent what kind of season he is having. The answer you may receive could make you believe that the opponent is a superwoman and that you can't possibly win.

Who Serves First

Service is determined either by having the referee toss a coin or by one of the players spinning a racquet. The winner has four choices: serve, receive, choose on which side to begin the match, or give the choice to the opponent. Unless you are unable to make decisions, don't give the opponent the choice.

Why Choose Side?

During the match, you and the opponent will change sides after every odd game. Thus, two of the first three games will be played on one side. There are four reasons to have that one-game advantage: First, if the angle of the sun is going to cause one player to look directly into the sun, you may wish to choose the other side. One of the pros I worked with couldn't stand to see his shadow on the court; he wanted the sun in front of him rather than behind him. Second, the background at the facility may be much better on one side. Third, the court may be in better condition on one side. Martina Navratilova always said the old Court One at Wimbledon was sloped on one side; I played a tournament where the court was sloped down and the first eleven games were won by the guy hitting downhill. Fourth, the wind may be prevailing from one side.

Why Choose to Serve?

If you have a weapon-grade serve, you should be confident that you will hold serve most of the day. In the 1997 Wimbledon, Sampras won the tournament, holding serve all but two games in seven rounds of play. By serving first, you start out ahead, and the opponent feels the constant pressure to hold just to get even. There's no margin for error in his struggle.

Why Choose to Return?

If your service return is one of the best parts of your game, choose to return first. If you can break serve right away, you may be able to take much of the fight out of the opponent.

If you're a slow or nervous starter, returning first gives you one additional game to settle down and ease into the match. It's nice to win every game; however, the opponent is supposed to hold serve some or all the time. If you lose the first game because the opponent holds serve, this should not negatively impact your game. After all, you are simply on serve.

The Warm-up

Match warm-up is a five-to-ten-minute period where you hit moderately to the opponent and ready your basic shots for the first game. The purpose of the warm-up is, not surprisingly, to warm up each other. You have an obligation to hit appropriate balls to the opponent so he, too, can warm up; you are not supposed to be practicing put-away shots. One of the least rational statements I hear from unseasoned players is that they fear that hitting directly back to the opponent in warm-up will cause them to do the same during the match. In practice, we work on directing the ball all the time. Three minutes of hitting the ball directly to the opponent should not override months of directional practice.

If you deliberately don't warm up, you're not fooling your opponent; you're shorting yourself, as it will instead take many actual games to ready yourself. Part of match strategy begins in warm-up, as you show your opponent your great shots. This adds to his pressure. First you warm up your ground strokes, then volleys, then overheads, then serve. On each of these skills you are showing your opponent why he should be afraid of your ability. Often the match is won in warm-up; if you cannot stay with me, you have no chance.

In the 1997 Sybase Tournament in San Jose, California, the number one player from Stanford, Ryan Wolters, played Andre Agassi in the first round. Wolters said that Agassi hit the ball harder in the warm-up than anyone he had ever played. Although Agassi was hitting toned-down shots, he had already won the match. He had, within the bounds of good sportsmanship and legitimate warm-up, scared his opponent to death.

The warm-up period includes serves. Once the match starts, play is continuous. Many young players like to wait for their first service game before they warm up their serves. This is against the rules. All practice serves must be taken before play begins. Make sure that you give your opponent an equal number of warm-up serves. You hit three serves, then the opponent hits three. If you fail to get a serve over the net after you have hit your third ball, toss the rest of the balls to the opponent. Don't take extra serves.

Computer On: Start Play

You must be ready to play at your learned level on the first point of the first game. All of your preparation, plus warm-up, must have readied you. The first games are important, for if you are a slow or lackadaisical starter, you risk the opponent's gaining control of the match.

You must begin an instant play analysis. Even if you have played today's opponent on several other occasions, today may be different. Observe what is working for you and what is not. If you are hitting well, keep it up. You can even juice up your hitting. Gustavo Kuerten, the 1997 French Open winner, said that during the finals he was hitting so well that he decided to hit even harder and still stayed in control. Try to understand how you are hurting your opponent and keep at it.

Unfortunately, for one of several reasons, you may be slightly off. Instead of insisting on firing your shots and missing, pull them in a bit; don't press for so much power or precision-aiming. You must remember that even at the highest level of pro tennis, most matches are lost, not won. So if you are not hitting well, at least make your opponent hit more shots. As the match progresses, you may find your rhythm improves, enabling you to go for more.

As quickly as possible, determine which of your opponent's shots and strategies are hurting you and calculate a solution. Young or unseasoned players may see shots they have never before encountered, while the experienced players quickly diagnose and counter problems. If you have the ability to curtail the damage that your opponent is inflicting, you have a chance to prevail.

Feel the Match

You need to develop a sense of when in the match to step up your game as much as you possibly can—that is, when the opponent is getting down and frustrated. When this is happening, play as aggressively as you can to finish off the opponent. If you win the first set, it is critical that you keep the pressure on, especially in the opening games of the second set. You may get the opponent to mentally and physically quit—having given a great effort in the first set and failing, he may convince himself to give up.

John Newcombe, the great Australian player and now a coach, said that you must sense when the top player is stepping up his gears and stay with him, or you've lost the match at that point. Particularly on big points, get ready for the step-up. If you are losing, try to keep the score as close as possible and not get discouraged. Often just by hanging tough, the pressure of the match could adversely affect your opponent and turn the match around. This is particularly true if you lost the first set. You may need to step up your game or make strategy adjustments, but don't be discouraged. When the match started, your goal was to win two sets, and losing this first set put you no farther from your goal.

When a match enters a third set, the opponent— at least on this day—has shown an ability to compete evenly with you. Don't be discouraged that the match has lasted this long. If you won the first set then lost the second, try to return to the formulas that won for you. If you feel the opponent has adjusted to you and now controls the match, you must readjust your strategy. If you had been serving and volleying and the opponent's return game improved, don't force the action; adjust and beat the opponent with your patience game.

If you won the second set to take the match to three, keep on doing what won the previous set for you. You have the momentum of the match, so keep running.

CHAPTER 11

Postmatch Analysis

After every match, win or lose, you should analyze what went right, wrong, and what needs to be improved upon. Then, during your practice sessions, work on the weak aspects of your game.

You Won

Each win should build your confidence that you can win pressure matches. You need an honest evaluation of what transpired. If your coach attended the match, review it and discuss the key elements. If you are by yourself, do the same analysis. From your experience in this match, what could you improve on to play better next time?

Even on the best day, no one is perfect. Learning to live without perfection is what tennis is about at the competitive level. If a certain part of your game was off, do some extra hitting or practicing so that you will feel confident going into the next match.

You Beat a Lesser Opponent

Congratulate yourself. A win is always a positive development. In most cases, the person you played was working on his game and trying very hard to win, so your win is a significant one. It's not your responsibility to make sure that the opponent is a quality opponent. If, through fortune, you were presented with a lesser opponent, that's the opponent's fault. Although it is easy to get dragged down, you did not.

Never moan about the score; the result is what is important. As Vince Lombardi used to ask, "Did you win, or did you lose?" One of my top boys used to moan after winning 6-3, 6-3. "I must be terrible; I should have won 6-1, 6-1." Recognize that you achieved your goal: winning.

In all sports, the formula for a great winning percentile is the same: always beat those below you, and play even with those above you. Many individuals and teams are only playing .500 ball; they play .500 ball with those above them, yet also with those below them. Consistently beating players you are supposed to beat is a skill you must master to achieve a winning percentile.

You Beat an Equal or Better Player

This a great win for you and will greatly increase your belief that you can hang with and beat the big players. The more big wins you earn, the less pressure you will feel in these situations. You have proven yourself.

New faces constantly emerge on the tennis scene. The key to a player's rise in the rankings is the big win. The more big wins a player earns, the more she moves to the top, and the more she belongs there. Each big win solidifies the player's newly gained ranking; as the confidence grows, the wins increase. Especially in close matches, the more winning experience you have, the more you will come through, creating a self-fulfilling prophecy.

Tournament Play

If you win, you get to play more matches. Each advance becomes a new experience, and as you progress you are bound to feel more pressure and nervousness. Hopefully, you will play enough tournaments so that the pressure becomes second nature. Even the pros talk about the increased pressure felt as they went farther in a tournament for the first time.

Getting through the last victory is very difficult. In the beginning of his career, Ivan Lendl was regarded as a loser because he failed in so many of his early finals. Once he broke through—winning the French Open in spectacular fashion, coming from down two sets to love against John McEnroe—he constantly won other majors and shook the loser label. In 1997 Patrick Rafter became one of the top three players in the world. He had lost the first six finals of that year before he broke through and won a tournament. So don't feel bad if it takes a while to bring home the first-place trophy.

If you have won a team or league match, you are done for the day! Congratulations. Absorb the confidence that winning a match brings to you. The more team or league matches you win, the more matches you *will* win—winning is contagious. If your teammates are still playing a match, it is very helpful and supportive of you to watch and cheer them on.

If you win a tournament match, you've earned the chance to play again. If time permits, and potential opponents are still playing, scout their matches—it's a big help to know what's coming next. If you will play a lefty, go hit some balls against a lefty. If you will play a big spin player, have your coach or a hitting buddy feed you balls with spin. Even if you can't scout on this day, hopefully you can deduce a scouting report from your previously played matches, or by talking to a friend who has played the opponent.

When you're scouting, you are looking to identify certain aspects of the opponent's game. What type of shots does he hit? What kind of spin? Is there spin variation on the ground strokes? What kind of serves does he hit? What is the quality of the first and second serve? Is there a mixture of spins? Is there a mixture of placement? What kind of net game does he have? What kind of game plan does the opponent use? Are there patterns in his shots and game plan? I also advise that you keep a record of the scouting report—you may play the opponent again or face an opponent similar to one you have scouted and played in the past.

You Lost

In a tournament, everyone except one player loses. Thus, in a draw of 128 players, there are 127 losers. As dominant as the likes of Connors, Lendl, and Sampras have been as the top players, in their great years they won only a quarter of the events in which they played.

You can shrug off some losses the second the match is over, but others stay with you a long time. John McEnroe says that his loss to Ivan Lendl in the finals of the French Open still haunts him. Losses aren't supposed to shake your confidence in yourself as a player, and with some losses, that's easy to accept; but for others, it's tough. You invested time, energy, and emotion, yet you lost, so it's understandable if you feel disappointed. Bounce back as quickly as you can; there are more matches to be played. Take comfort knowing that at one time or another, everyone who has ever played serious, competitive tennis wished that they could break all of their racquets and never play again.

You Lost to a Lesser Player

You know that you are a better player than your opponent, but for a variety of reasons, you didn't bring your best to the court. This is a tough loss to deal with, because your practice and match preparation were not supposed to let this happen. This kind of loss can carry over, leading to a lack of confidence during the next match, sending you on a downward cycle.

If you are losing to lesser players, it is time for an honest evaluation of your game. In practice, something in your preparation is not working, and you must start experimenting with your routines to see what must be added or subtracted to help you play at your learned level when it counts. Particularly if a part of your game that you've been working on failed, you don't yet own the skills, and more work must be done.

The Match Slipped Away

Regardless of the quality of the opponent today, the match was yours for the taking. Often the match changed on a key point or game. Instead of finishing off the opponent, you let him back into the match, and with renewed life he stole the victory.

The serious problem with this type of loss is that when you again get into a position to win, you may start to feel a lack of confidence because of the prior failure. If this happens more than a couple times, as the end approaches you may be filled with a feeling of "Here we go again." There's no question that you can't make a habit of letting matches escape from you.

In practice you must set up more situations in which you are in the lead and must work on closing out the win. Play music during practice to create a distraction, and learn to focus better during those periods. Many times not finishing off matches is a matter of not being as focused as is necessary.

Loss of Opportunity

Sometimes a loss has consequences in your mind that are far greater than the match itself. If your ranking could have gone way up with a win, or you had been aiming to beat a certain opponent, it is not unusual to have a major letdown. When you play next you may still be so disappointed that you start to cycle downward. You must work out the disappointment during practice, realizing that there will be other chances—bury this feeling through hard work. You need to believe that you will get that opponent next time.

The Opponent Won a Closely Fought Battle

This happens. You played well, but the opponent played better. At the 1997 U.S. Open, Sampras lost to Korda 7-6 in the fifth set of a match well played by both players. Sampras said that obviously he was disappointed about not winning, but he wasn't going to lose any sleep over it. All you can ask of yourself on any given day is to play the way you have been trained: 80 percent of the time, that will do the job. Once in a while, though, you will meet an opponent who is just slightly hotter and can actually win the match on his own. This isn't a loss to feel bad about, because you did your job. The lesson to be learned is that you need to play a few points tougher. In any close match, two key points could make a difference. At those key moments, you must be better at stepping up your game to another level.

At times a match like this can greatly encourage you because you fully realize that you played well against a good opponent. All of your hard work is starting to pay off—you are closing the gap between the top players and you. At any tier in tennis, believing that you belong on the court with the opponent and can win is the key. If you can get close to winning against a top player, you can push it to the next level and start to prevail.

In practice, keep on doing what has worked so well, but try to push yourself to develop a little more mental toughness to help you win these tight matches.

You Got Killed

Appreciate that the opponent is much more advanced and prepared than you and presents a good role model for your growth. This level of play should inspire you to work harder at becoming better—and now you can see how good "better" really is. The danger of getting killed is that seeing the gap between you and the opponent may discourage you from working hard because you may feel it's impossible to reach the opponent's level. The wonderful aspect of tennis is that although you may never reach that same level, you can still reach a great level of play. Don't be discouraged by this loss. Just continue working on becoming the best player you can.

In practice, work on closing the gap in your and your opponents' skill levels. This may require new techniques for your shots and a much better mastery of your game strategies.

Returning to Practice

When the matches are over, it's time to go back to work. The common question, though, is how soon. There are times when you should take a break for a short period.

If you have been playing many weeks in a row, even playing very well and winning most of the time, you should take a few days off now and then. Especially after a tough loss, it is productive to take off a few mental-health days, giving yourself time to calm down and not have the loss eat at you.

You also need additional rest time when you're injured. Everyone's pain level is different. Finishing off matches that you have started is often a very courageous thing to do when you are slightly injured. However, even if you are ninety years old, you have more tennis days coming. Playing on and further injuring yourself isn't something that is going to advance your progress. When the match is over, the decision to go back to practice needs to be based on the reality of whether the practice time will be well spent. When your body parts are ailing, you must listen to them and give them time to heal. To a certain extent, everyone is hurt a little all the time. Learn to recognize which pain is controllable, which you can play through, and which will not let you perform.

As you return to the practice court, take with you the lessons learned in your match play and continue to work on striving to improve. As great as you get, there is always room for growth.

All serious players need to work on their game all the time. Of the many elements of the game to learn, Sampras's continual quest to improve is one of the greatest for us all to emulate. Even though he has been a great winner for years, winning his first Grand Slam at age nineteen, he has continued to work on and add to his game. Even when you are winning, you must still strive to improve your game.

Conclusion

The key to success is to continue to grow, and winning is not the only marker for that. The more you learn and grow as a player, the sooner you will earn more wins. Sampras was not a great winner as a junior player because he played higher than his age group all the time. This made him improve at a faster rate, but it did not lead to winning many junior tournaments. There's no question that some players can tolerate the losses better than others. If you need to gain some confidence, schedule some easier opponents to play during practice. It's unhealthy to continue losing so frequently that you feel you are no longer able to win. Don't let losing destroy your interest in learning more and playing the game.

When you start to doubt your direction, then it's time to return to your practice sessions to reflect on and reexamine your goals. The key elements of practice in this book that I have presented are mandatory pieces in the growth process, but how you fill in these pieces may change from time to time. You may need to reexamine your coaching, or perhaps your work schedule needs a different balance. Reevaluate the process to see what is required for you to believe that you are on the right track to achieving the desired growth.

Seriously reevaluate the goals you have set for yourself. While there are many rungs on the tennis ladder, all of them have significant value. The fact that you may not reach the rung you were shooting for doesn't make you a failure.

Parental Goals and Junior Achievements

Although it may seem like a good idea to have your twelve- to eighteen-year-old child support you financially, it's not: it places tremendous and unnecessary stress on the child. If the goal of the family is to make the junior a world-class pro, but the losses clearly indicate that this is unrealistic, then you must seriously assess the goal. At age ten, there are one hundred thousand juniors around the world who look as if they may become, in time, great pros. By the time these juniors are eighteen years old, only one hundred are left. Of those one hundred, maybe half will make a good living playing pro tennis. There are one hundred and fifty players on each of the men's and women's tour earning a living. Those jobs are currently taken; each year maybe twenty new people are able to crack into the top one hundred and fifty. The odds are extremely long that your junior will be one of the handful who makes it big.

Some don't make it to the top because they were not really that good, some get hurt, some lose interest, some don't have the heart or fortitude. Not being able to make the pro tour doesn't preclude shooting for a college scholarship. Playing college tennis is a huge achievement. The key element to understand is that losing in a growth environment isn't detrimental as long as losing doesn't destroy confidence. The junior and the parent must not emotionally beat up the junior for losing. Don't let losing crush interest.

In this book, I have presented the structure you need to follow to become a focused, serious student of the game. I have shown you how to practice, how to prepare for matches, how to play the match, and how to return to practice after the match. If you follow the plans laid out in this book, you will have a clear roadmap for your pursuit of tennis excellence. No one knows how good he or she may become at any activity. However, having clear goals and structure on how to achieve those goals will enable you to become as good as you possibly can. Tennis is a great sport with a lifetime of rewards. Reap the fullest benefits possible from your pursuits.

Acknowledgment

On May 3, 1996, one of my best friends, Tim Gullikson, died from inoperable brain cancer at age forty-four. I knew Tim for over thirty years. We played tennis together as kids in Wisconsin junior tournaments. Tim was a true friend, a mentor, and a great inspiration in my life and the lives of many others. Tim's playing career, along with that of his twin brother, Tom, developed after he graduated from college. As a playing pro Tim had a very successful career, winning four singles titles and sixteen doubles titles, ten of them with Tom. He reached a career-high ranking of eighteen in 1978. But he had even greater success as a pro coach. Starting with Barbara Potter, Tim coached Martina Navratilova, Aaron Krickstein, and finally Pete Sampras on a full-time basis.

In 1986 on Court Eighteen at the U.S. Open, I ran into Tim watching a match. Over the prior fourteen years I had seen both brothers on occasion as I went to various tournaments. We talked for twenty minutes that day and renewed our friendship. Tim was about to retire as a player and begin his career as a coach. From that point on, Tim let me have a window of opportunity that few will ever have. I was allowed to be a small part of his work. Tim freely shared information with me and on occasion even asked my advice. The two most unique parts of the program I teach, my play program and toss system, I invented from the work I was able to share with Tim. For those times I will be forever grateful.

In any field there are very few who can perform their jobs in a great manner. Tim was one of a handful who was truly a great coach. Aaron Krickstein told me that the reason he liked Tim was that Tim was not afraid to tell him what had to be done. In a time, in all pro sports, when the coached are often uncoachable, the ability of the coach to have the respect of the coached is disappearing. I know that all those whom Tim touched had a great respect for his talents, and thus they listened. Pete Sampras went from number six to number one, with the possibility of being the best player ever, under Tim's tutelage.

Anywhere we went with Tim there were many people around him, and all considered him a friend. His outgoing personality and lust for life were contagious. It was my great hope, as it was the hope of many others, that if any person could beat back the unbeatable, Tim could. He did for eighteen months. Every time we talked he was positive, spiritually sound, and upbeat about his chances of winning his battle against cancer. The last time we talked was eleven days before he died. We talked about the importance of staying alive for another year and a half because so much progress was being made in cancer research. He said that was going to be no problem. Until the end he fought as he lived, with a great lust for life. I feel greatly privileged to have known Tim. My life was enriched by having him as a friend.

Index

A

adhesive tape, 88–89

adult players, 6, 8, 11–12

Agassi, Andre, 4, 53, 60

    conditioning and, 63–64

    double bounce and, 115–16

    forehand of, 33

    mental conditioning and, 71, 75, 76

    patience zone and, 54

    use of bandanna, 88

    in warm-up, 98, 122

anger, 79

apparel, 89–90

approach shots, 51

Ashe, Arthur, 60

A Stopwatch, 77

ATP tour, 78

attack zones, 52, 53

attitude, 19, 22–25, 72–74

Australian Open, 63, 68, 72, 73, 87

B

back foot position, 43

backhand

    position for, 28

    short shots, 37, *37*

    start technique, *30*, 31

    volley, 38, *38*

bad habits, 16

bags, 83–90

balance, 35–36, 57, 75–76

balls. *See* tennis balls

Bancroft racquets, 84, 85

Band-Aids, 88–89

baseball, 20, 80, 94

baseline, 54–55, 56

baseline-wall strategy, 57–59

basketball, 5, 10, 52, 77, 81, 99
Becker, Boris, 11, 23, 48,
72, 92
Berasategui, Alberto, 28
body language, 110–11
Bruguera, Sergi, 55
B Stopwatch, 75

C
caffeine, 69
Cash, Pat, 65
Chang, Michael, 55, 58, 84
chess, 47
children, 67
choking, 111–12
choosing sides, 120
clay court surfaces, 91–92,
113, 114
clothes, 96
clothes bags, 89–90
club teams, 11
coaches, 1, 2, 24
attending matches, 117
becoming your own coach, 17
conditioning, 64
finding, 3–5
learning process and, 2–3
prematch rituals and, 98
college tennis, 6, 10, 11, 135
concentration, 15–17
conditioning, 10, 12, 16, 63–64
food intake, 67–69
loss of, 13–14
mental, 71–81
off-court, 66–67
practice drills, 65–66
rest, 69
conditioning time, 7
confidence, 1

Connors, Jimmy, 1, 60, 79, 128
conversion rate, 108
Corretja, Alex, 67, 73
Costa, Albert, 101
Courier, Jim, 33, 50, 53, 73
conditioning and, 63–64
on Sampras, 105
short hits and, 59
court surfaces, 91–93
cramping, 96
cross-country running, 10
crosscourt shots, 51
crowds, 116–17

D
dance classes, 66
Davis, Marty, 4
Davis Cup, 59
default-time rules, 97
deuce point, 106
diet. *See* food intake
disputes, 115–16
distractions, xi–xii, 79, 116–17
Dodge, Larry, 75–76
double bounces, 115–16
down-pacing strategy, 60–62
drinks, 68, 69, 89

E
Edberg, Stefan, 28, 49, 79, 92, 111
emotions, handling, 74, 79
energy boosters, 68–69
Enqvist, Thomas, 45
errors, 110, 111
excuses, 109–17
expression, 19

F
fall-back jump shot, 55

family members, 117, 134–35
fighting drills, 65
finish technique, 33, *34–35*
fitness, 7
fluid replacement, 68, 96
food intake, 67–69
football, 80–81
footwork, 66
forehand
  position for, 28
  short shots, 37, *37*
  start technique, 29, *29*
  tomahawk slice, 36, *36*
  volley, 38, *38*
fortitude, 80–81, 134
four-zones strategy, 50–57
French Open, 4, 18, 43, 61, 71, 122
  clay court surfaces at, 92

G
game plan, 24, 47
  baseline wall, 57–59
  down-pacing, 60–62
  hitting short, 59–60
  playing four zones, 50–57
  serve and volley, 48–50
game points, 106–7
Garrison, Zina, 87
Gilbert, Brad, 60–61
goal levels, 13
golf, 112
Graf, Steffi, 74, 79, 112
Grand Slam tournaments, 4, 8,
  81, 132
grass court surfaces, 92
grinding, 71
grip, 27–29
ground strokes, 44–45, 53, 121
Gullikson, Tim, 14, 16, 53, 73, 74

H
hand position, 28–29
hard courts, 92–93
Har-Tru court surfaces, 91, 93,
  113, 114
hats, 96
"having the elbow," 111
headbands, 88
higher-ranked opponents, 101–2
Hingis, Martina, 57
hit point, 32
hitting short, 59–60
hitting shots, 98
Hoveler, Charles, 18

I
injuries, 99, 132
instruction, 2–5
Italian Open, 105
Ivanisevic, Goran, 116

J
Jee, Mark, 21, 67
Jensen, Luke, 98
Johnson, Magic, 15
jumping rope, 66
junior players
  parental goals and, 134–35
  work schedule for, 6, 9–11

K
Korda, Petr, 109, 130
Kuerten, Gustavo, 122

L
Laver, Rod, 96
lead tape, 89
learning, building-block
  process of, 17

Lendl, Ivan, 50, 63, 127, 128
lights, 94–95
line calls, 113–15
liquids. *See* drinks
Loehr, Jim, 8–9
losing
    attitude toward, 21–22
    junior players and, 135
    postmatch analysis and,
        128–31
lower-ranked opponents, 102
Luther, Dave, 21, 27

M
Martin, Todd, 89
matches, 119–24
    court surface, 91–93
    going to, 97
    key concepts, 105–17
    opponents, 101–3
    postmatch analysis, 125–32
    prematch rituals, 97–101
    preparation for, 83–90
    weather conditions, 93–96
MatchMate racquets, 84
match points, 108–9
McEnroe, John, 4, 11,
        43, 84
    distractions and, 116
    at French Open, 92, 127, 128
    on game plans, 47
    on game plan strategy, 53
    on losing, 128
    sportsmanship and, 115
    stringing and, 86
    at U.S. Open, 97
men's tennis, 4, 134
mental conditioning, 71, 100–1
    attitude, 72–74

heart and fortitude,
        80–81
    state of mind, 74–80
minitennis, 60
missing shots, 20–21, 79
mistakes, learning from, 20
Moya, Carlos, 44
music, 2, 130
Muster, Thomas, 55, 84–85, 113

N
Navratilova, Martina, 68, 120
NCAA championship, 11
Newcombe, John, 123
Newsweek ATP tournament, 19
not-up shots, 115
Novotna, Jana, 111–112

O
off-court conditioning, 66–67
one-on-one drills, 65
opponents
    challenging calls and, 114
    conversation with, 119
    as excuse for your poor play,
        112–13
    known, 102–3
    postmatch analysis and, 126–131
    respect for, 23, 72, 73
    unknown, 101–2
opportunity, loss of, 130
overgrips, 88
overheads, 32, *32*, 121
overhitting, 72
overreactions, 110–11
overtraining, 13

P
parallax, 113

patience drills, 65
patience zone, 54
penalty points, 117
performance level, 24–25
periodization, 13–14
personal trainers, 7
Philippoussis, Mark, 117
pitch-and-catch drills, 65
playing sets, 65
points, importance of, 105–6
postmatch analysis, 125–32
practice, 15–25, 133–34
    goals of, 1–14
    mental conditioning and, 79, 81
    returning to after matches,
        131–32
    shot mechanics and, 45
    winning attitude and, 73–74
prematch rituals, 97–101
present tense, 77–78
pressure, 127
pro circuit, 6
pull-up ground strokes, 44–45
put-way shots, 121

Q
quiet time, 98–99

R
racquets, 84–86
Rafter, Patrick, 127
rebreaking, 107
referees, 119
Reneberg, Richey, 11, 19
rest time, 69, 132
retooling, 45
returning serves, 120–21
rhythm, 33, 61
Rios, Marcelo, 43

Rios Motion, 43–44, *44*
rubberized court surfaces, 92

S
Safin, Marat, 59
Sampras, Pete, 4, 7, 8, 16, 48, 111
    early-round play of, 105
    endorsement for Nike shoes, 87
    food/drink consumption and,
        67–68
    forehand of, 33
    at French Open, 92, 101
    Grand Slam tournaments and, 81,
        132
    grip and, 28
    handling of emotional stress, 74
    as junior player, 133
    on losing, 130
    overgrips and, 88
    on practice, 18, 21
    proportion of victories, 128
    racquets and, 85, 89
    responses to incoming shots, 78
    serving techniques of, 39, *40*, 43,
        45, 56
    stringing and, 86
    at U.S. Open, 130
    at Wimbledon, 109, 120
    winning attitude and, 72, 73
schedules, matches and, 100
scores, 123–24
Seles, Monica, 28, 59, 79
service breaks, 107
service square area, 50–51
serving, 39–44, *40–42, 44*
    determining first serve, 119–20
    hand position and, 28–29
    serve-and-volley strategy, 48–50
    serve-return technique, 8

serving (*continued*)
   serve stances, 4
set points, 107–8
shadows, 94
shoes/shoelaces, 87
short shots, 37, *37*
shot mechanics, 27, 36–38, *36–38*
   balance, 35–36
   finish technique, 33, *34–35*
   grip, 27–29
   hit point, 32
   mental conditioning and, 76
   practice and, 45
   pull-up ground strokes, 44–45
   rhythm, 33
   serving, 39–44, *40–42, 44*
   start technique, 29, *29–32*, 31, 32
shoulders and hip rotation, 43
shower facilities, 90
sighting the ball, 75–76
skills, mastery of, 17–19, 129
soccer, 10
sports, 5, 10
sports injuries, 99
sportsmanship, 113, 115, 122
sprint work, 66
stair climbers, 66
start technique, 29, *29–32*, 31, 32
state of mind, 74–80
Stefnaki, Larry, 43
step-up shots, 53, 123
strength workouts, 10, 67
stretching, 9, 10, 66–67
stringing, 86
sunlight, 93–94, 120
Super Nine, 4

T
talent, 80, 81

Tarango, Jeff, 113
team matches, 97
television commentators, 8
temperature, 86, 95–96
tennis
   compared to baseball, 20
   compared to basketball, 52, 77
   compared to chess, 47
   development in, 14
   learning in, 2–3
   match play, 83
   videotapes and, 8–9
tennis balls, 89, 95, 96, 110, 116
   chasing, 76
   repositioning after hitting, 77
   sighting, 75
ten-point servers, 65
tomahawk slice, 36, *36*
topspin, 32, 59
tossing arm motion, 40–43, *41–42*
touch shots, 51
touring pros, 2, 3, 17, 135
tournament play, 127–28
towels, 87–88
track, 10, 66
treadmills, 66
two-on-one drills, 65, 73

U
umpires, 114–15, 116
underspin, 20, 32
U.S. Open, 4, 7, 67, 74, 84, 87
   hard court surfaces at, 93
   lights at, 94
USTA, 6, 12

V
Vicario, Arantxa Sánchez, 61
videotapes, 8–9, 11, 12, 67

visual learning, 7–8
volleys, 38, *38*
   hand position for, 29, 31, *31*
   serve and, 48–50
   in warm-up, 121

W
walking, 66
warm-ups, 121–22
Washington, MaliVai, 11
water, 68
weather conditions,
   93–96
weight training, 67
weight transfer, 42
Wilkerson, John, 98
Wimbledon, 60, 71, 92

wind, 95, 120
winning
   attitude for, 22–23, 72–74,
     99–100, 112
   postmatch analysis and,
     125–28
Wolters, Ryan, 122
women's tennis, 4, 134
Woodbridge, Todd, 45
Woodforde, Mark, 72, 75
Woods, Tiger, 33
work ethic, 23
workout programs, 66
work schedules, 5–6
   adult players, 11–12
   juniors, 9–11
wristbands, 88